15, 165   9,95

S0-BIP-221

OTHER INQUISITIONS

The Texas Pan American Series

Other Inquisitions 1937–1952

BY JORGE LUIS BORGES

TRANSLATED BY RUTH L. C. SIMMS

INTRODUCTION BY JAMES E. IRBY

UNIVERSITY OF TEXAS PRESS, AUSTIN

The Texas Pan American Series is published with the assistance of
a revolving publication fund established by the Pan American
Sulphur Company. Publication of this book was assisted also by a
grant from the Rockefeller Foundation through the Latin American
translation program of the Association of American University
Presses.

International Standard Book Number 0-292-73322-4 (cloth)
International Standard Book Number 0-292-76002-7 (paper)
Library of Congress Catalog Card Number 64-19416
Copyright © 1964 by the University of Texas Press
Copyright © 1965 by Jorge Luis Borges
All rights reserved
Printed in the United States of America

Third Paperback Printing, 1988

Requests for permission to reproduce material from this work
should be sent to Permissions, University of Texas Press,
Box 7819, Austin, Texas 78713-7819.

To Margot Guerrero

INTRODUCTION

This work, here translated into English for the first time, is Borges' best collection of essays, and forms a necessary complement to the stories of *Ficciones* and *El Aleph*, which have made him famous. *Otras inquisiciones* was first published in 1952, but its pieces had appeared separately (most of them in Victoria Ocampo's review *Sur* or in the literary supplement of *La Nación*) over the preceding thirteen years. The title harks back to Borges' first volume of essays, published in 1925, when he was twenty-six. Those original *Inquisiciones* now seem to him affected and dogmatic *avant-garde* exercises; he will not have the book reprinted and buys up old copies to destroy them. The present collection's curiously ancillary title is therefore ambiguous and ironic. "Other" can mean "more of the same": more efforts doomed to eventual error, perhaps, but certainly more quests or inquiries into things, according to the etymology. But "other" is also "different," perhaps even "opposite": these essays hardly set forth inflexible dogma, with their sagacious heresies, pursuit of multiple meanings, and dubitative style. In 1925 Borges stated that his title aimed to dissociate "inquisition" once and for all from monks' cowls and the smoke of damnation. After an inquisitorial pursuit of his own work, the effort continues.

Borges' reference to De Quincey in opening the essay on John Donne is typical in its candid confession of influence and also typical in the English and uncommon nature of that influence. For *Otras inquisiciones* will probably seem no less unusual to the English-speaking than to the Spanish-speaking reader. Traits of nineteenth-century essayists as little read today as De Quincey—whimsical bookishness, a blend of conversational discursiveness and elevated diction, informal opinion prevailing over formal analysis—combine with the many unfamiliar subjects to produce a kind of alienation effect, a somewhat archaic or even atemporal quality remote from our age of urgent involvements, as well as from current critical modes. This effect is more compounded than mitigated by a very un-nineteenth-century brevity that may seem fragmentary and, with the great heterogeneity of the subjects, make the collection appear arbitrary and without unity. But there is method here; its basic principle is already suggested by the union of diverse and opposite meanings in the title.

One of the foremost quests in *Otras inquisiciones* is for symmetries; two that are rediscovered throughout the book under various guises appear in the first two essays. In "The Wall and the Books" Borges evokes the Chinese emperor who both created the Great Wall and wanted all books prior to him burned. This enormous mystification inexplicably "satisfies" and, at the same time, "disturbs" Borges. His purpose then is to seek the reasons for "that emotion." (Note that the stimulus for the supposedly cerebral Borges is not an idea, that the satisfaction and disturbance are *one* feeling.) Various conjectures lead him to suggest that the aesthetic phenomenon consists in the "imminence of a revelation that is not yet produced": a kind of expanding virtuality of thought, an unresolved yet centrally focussed multiplicity of views, which the essay's form as discussion, as tacit dialogue, has already reflected. The other essays also display, centrally or laterally, paradoxes or oppositions with analogous overtones. At the end of "Avatars of the Tortoise" the paradoxes of Zeno and the antinomies of Kant indicate for Borges that the universe is ultimately a dream, a product of the mind, unreal because free of the apparent limits of time and space we call "real." But the paradoxical confession with which "New Refutation of Time" ends—"it [time] is a fire that consumes me, but I am the fire"—must conclude that "the world, alas, is real; I, alas, am Borges." Extremes of fantastic hope and skepticism paradoxically coexist in Borges' thought.

In "Pascal's Sphere" he examines an image which is not only paradoxical in itself—the universe as an infinite sphere, in other words, a boundless form perfectly circumscribed—but which has also served to express diametrically opposite emotions: Bruno's elation and Pascal's anguish. But the other basic symmetry to note here is Borges' history of the metaphor. Not only paradoxes are found throughout this collection, but also various listings of ideas or themes or images which though diverse in origin and detail are essentially the same. In "The Flower of Coleridge" the coincidence of Valéry's, Emerson's, and Shelley's conceptions of all literature as the product of one Author seems itself to bear out that conception. At the beginning of the essay on Hawthorne, Borges again briefly traces the history of a metaphor—the likening of our dreams to a theatrical performance —and adds that true metaphors cannot be invented, since they have always existed. Such "avatars" point beyond the flux and diversity of history to a realm of eternal archetypes, which, though limited in number, "can be all things for all people, like the Apostle." While the paradox upsets our common notions of reality and suggests that irreducible elements are actually one, recurrence negates history and the separateness of individuals. Of course, this too is a paradox, as "New Refutation of Time" shows: time must exist in order to provide the successive identities with which it is to be "refuted." The two symmetries noted above, if we pursue their implications far enough, finally coalesce, with something of the same dizzying sense, so frequent in Borges' stories, of infinite permutations lurking at every turn. Both are uses of what he calls a pantheist extension of the principle of identity—God is all things: a suitably heterogeneous selection of these may allude to Totality—which has, as he notes in the essay on Whitman, unlimited rhetorical possibilities.

Stylistic uses of that principle are the paradoxical or near-paradoxical word pairs ("that favors or tolerates another interpretation," "our reading of Kafka refines and changes our reading of the poem") and also the ellipses and transferred epithets based on substitution of part for whole, whose possibilities for animation of the abstract and impersonal explain why Borges terms a typical example "allegorical" at the beginning of "From Allegories to Novels." (The classical concept of Literature's precedence over individuals, outlined in the first essay on Coleridge, is analogous to this and to the priority of archetypes. As we shall see, Borges' very personal essayistic manner actually reinforces such impersonality.) In general, the enumeration of sharply diverse yet somehow harmonizing parts that allude to some larger, static whole unnamable by any unilateral means is a common procedure underlying many features of Borges' style and form: the sentences that abruptly rotate their angular facets like cut stones, the succinct little catalogs that may comprise paragraphs and even whole essays, the allusions and generalizations that find echoes of the line of argument elsewhere and project it onto other planes, the larger confrontations of a writer with his alter ego (in himself or in another) or of the essay with its own revision or complement—all those series and inlays, in short, which are so much the curt mosaic design of this collection.

It is even possible to see the miscellaneous range of subjects taken up in *Otras inquisiciones* as yet another extension of the same "pantheist" principle, as the record of a random series of discoveries in books that variously point to one subsistent order beyond. In Borges' stories (as also in *Don Quixote*) the turning points, the crucial revelations, are very often marked by the finding of some unexpected text. *Otras inquisiciones* opens with the words "I read, not long ago . . ." and closes with the author's reflections on rereading his own essays. This ubiquitousness of books and their scrutiny is but one aspect of that ancient *topos*, with all its Cabalist elaborations, that so fascinates Borges: the world as Book, reality transmuted into Word, into intelligible Sign. *All* reality, including the symbolic and lived aspects we normally consider separate—the translation of this unity into literary form, as "Partial Enchantments of the *Quixote*" points out, is the structure of work within work in Cervantes' novel, in *Hamlet*, in *Sartor Resartus*, where the boundaries between fiction and life shift and tend to disappear.

Concentric structures of this kind abound in *Ficciones* and *El Aleph*, as do direct premonitions and echoes of those stories' themes in *Otras inquisiciones*. It is easy to see, for example, that the literary games of Tlön that attribute dissimilar works to the same writer and conjecture upon the apocryphal mentality thus obtained, like Pierre Menard's art of "the deliberate anachronism and the erroneous attribution," are only somewhat more extravagant applications of the scrutinies practiced in the essays. In fact, Borges' entire work, filled with recurring variants of the same interlocking themes, is a cento of itself, a repeated approximation of archetypes like those he glimpses in others. But a more intriguing comparison between his essays and his stories can be posed in this question: what is the difference for him between one genre and the other? Are his many fictions that masquerade as essays, such as "Tlön, Uqbar, Orbis Tertius" or "Pierre Menard, Author of the *Quixote,*" distinct from the "real" essays of *Otras inquisiciones* simply because the stories have invented books and authors as their subjects? But the fiction entitled "Story of the Warrior and the Captive" (in *El Aleph*) contains no invented element, save the speculative elaboration upon the scant facts of its real characters' lives, and the germs of this are found also in an essay like "The Enigma of Edward FitzGerald," with the same weighing of conjectures, bipartite structure, and final identity of figures greatly separate in time and place. The real difference seems to be one of emphasis or degree: fiction and fact, imagination and critique, are aspects of the same continuum throughout Borges' work, both within genres and among them. Hence, in these essays, he can use historical deeds to investigate the aesthetic phenomenon, to remark that the "inventions of philosophy are no less fantastic than those of art," to find in his own work a tendency to "evaluate religious or philosophical ideas on the basis of their aesthetic worth," and to add epilogues and afterthoughts that are the beginnings of those Chinese-box structures where literature devours and extends itself without limit.

Borges' major world-pictures have already been noted here in passing: the world as Book, the idealist and pantheist notions of the world as idea or dream, either man's or God's. (The Gnostic image suggested in the essay on John Donne—the world infinitely degraded, infinitely remote from God's perfection—is but the exact obverse of pantheism. As Borges observed in his earlier book *Discusión,* "what greater glory for a God than to be absolved of the world?") That these conceptions also coalesce is shown by the remark "we (the undivided divinity that operates within us) have dreamed the world" in "Avatars of the Tortoise," by the concluding sentence of "From Someone to Nobody," which suggests that all history is a dream of recurrent forms, and by the entire essay "The

Mirror of the Enigmas," with its "hieroglyphic" interpretation of the universe that Borges claims most befits "the intellectual God of the theologians," the infinite mind that can instantly grasp the most intricate figure in space and time (a nightmare of *ars combinatoria,* of pure chance) as a harmonious design. Borges' world-pictures all seem to join in postulating that the world is a supreme mind about to emerge from its symbols and reveal the unity of all things and beings *sub specie aeternitatis.*

But does Borges *believe* in such incredible cosmologies? Clearly not: the alternative of infinite chaos is also always about to emerge. The word "believe" here takes on the same uncertainty as "fiction" and "reality." His cosmologies are like hypotheses, cherished but also incurably problematical, as the whole tentative, self-critical cast of his style, at its most elaborate in "New Refutation of Time," indicates. Such flexibility of mind he finds lacking in his former idol Quevedo, who is immune to the charm of fantastic doctrines that are "probably false," and relishes in the atheist Omar Khayyām, who could interpret the Koran with strict orthodoxy and invoke in his studies of algebra the favor of "the God Who perhaps exists," because "every cultivated man is a theologian, and faith is not a requisite." Any theme set forth by Borges will be refuted by him somewhere else: the concept of autonomous pure form espoused in "The Wall and the Books" and "Quevedo" is rejected in the first paragraphs of the essay on Bernard Shaw. Self-refutation has, besides the virtues of probity, its advantages, its "apparent desperations and secret assuagements." One could suspect that Borges' nature, like Chesterton's, is a discord, and see these essays simply as its testimony, but it seems more accurate to consider *Otras inquisiciones* as a mask, as consciously projecting the image of a "possible poet," after the manner he has noted in Whitman and Valéry, those poetic personifications of fervor and intellect, each of whom is a counterpart of Borges' creative self (the former fully as much as the latter, contrary to widespread belief).

The nature and purpose of that projection are implied in three passages from scattered essays of Borges. In 1927 he called metaphysics "the only justification and finality of any theme." In 1933 he spoke of Icelandic kennings that produce "that lucid perplexity

xiv

which is the sole honor of metaphysics, its remuneration, and its source." And in 1944 he admired the "dialectical skill" of a fragment from Heraclitus, which insinuates part of its meaning and "gives us the illusion of having invented it." The themes of *Otras inquisiciones,* as such, matter less than the state of awareness their immediacy and strangeness and scope can induce. In Borges' sense, metaphysics is not an abstruse specialty, but the quotidian acts of all our thought, pursued to their consequences and revealed as the wonders they are. All ideas are arbitrary, fantastic, and useful. They should be remembered if forgotten or obscure, subverted if sacred (another form of oblivion), made absurd if banal—all for the sake of intelligence, of perceptibility. Borges' curious erudition, plausible paradoxes, and restless scrutinies serve those functions, as does his very readable style (that worn epithet must be revived and used here). Taut and effortless, transparent and mannered, deeply true to the genius of the Spanish language yet heterodox, his rhetoric is also a silent parody and extension of itself. For even certain excesses, the abruptness of certain transitions, the dubiousness of certain obviously sentimental attachments, seem a willful demonstration of the limits of his writing and thought, as if to invite the reader, once he is sufficiently initiated (Borges' work is never hermetic and is always intended for the reader), to "improve" upon these somewhat Socratic schemes. The *activation* of thought, shared by author and reader, miraculously effected over fatal distance and time by words whose sense alters and yet lives on, is the real secret promise of the infinite dominion of mind, not its images or finalities, which are expendable. This is the "method" of Borges' essays, the process both examined and enacted in them, received and passed on, as part of a great chain of being. Hence the essay on Whitman, hence the final epigraph from the seventeenth-century German mystic Angelus Silesius:

> *Freund, es ist auch genug. Im Fall du mehr willst lesen,*
> *So geh und werde selbst die Schrift und selbst das Wesen.*

Friend, this is enough. If you want to read more,
Go and be yourself the letter and the spirit.

JAMES E. IRBY

Princeton

CONTENTS

OTHER INQUISITIONS

The Wall and the Books

He, whose long wall the wand'ring
Tartar bounds....
Dunciad, II, 76.

I read not long ago that the man who ordered the building of the almost infinite Chinese Wall was the first Emperor, Shih Huang Ti, who also decreed the burning of all the books that had been written before his time. The fact that the two vast undertakings—the construction of five or six hundred leagues of stone to ward off the barbarians, and the rigorous abolition of history, or rather, of the past—had proceeded from the same person and had come to be regarded as expressions of his character, unaccountably satisfied and, at the same time, disturbed me. To investigate the reasons for that emotion is the purpose of this note.

Historically speaking, there is nothing abstruse in the two measures. Shih Huang Ti, King of Tsin, who lived at the time of the wars of Hannibal, conquered the Six Kingdoms and put an end to the feudal system. He built the wall, because walls were defenses; he burned the books because his opponents were invoking them to praise the emperors who had preceded him. Burning books and erecting fortifications are the usual occupations of princes; Shih Huang Ti was unusual in the scale on which he worked. At any rate, that is the opinion of some Sinologists, but I believe those two acts are more than an exaggeration or hyperbole of trivial orders. It commonly occurs that an orchard or a garden is enclosed within a wall, but not a whole empire. Nor is it a small matter to induce the most traditional of races to renounce the memory of its mythical or real past. The Chinese had had three thousand years of chronology (and during those years, the Yellow Emperor and Chuang-tze and Confucius and Lao-tzu) when Shih Huang Ti ordered that history should begin with him.

Shih Huang Ti had exiled his mother because she was a libertine; the orthodox saw nothing but impiety in his stern justice. Perhaps Shih Huang Ti wanted to destroy the canonical books because they were his accusers; perhaps Shih Huang Ti wanted to abolish the whole past in order to abolish a single memory: the memory of his mother's dishonor. (It was not unlike the case of a king in Judea who, seeking to kill one child, ordered that all children should be killed.) That is a valid conjecture, but it tells us nothing of the wall, the other aspect of the myth. According to historians, Shih Huang Ti forbade the mention of death and searched for the elixir of immortality. He became a recluse in a figurative palace, which had as many rooms as the number of days in the year. Those facts suggest that the wall in space and the fire in time were magic barriers to halt death. Baruch Spinoza has written that all things desire the continuance of their being; perhaps the Emperor and his magicians believed that immortality was intrinsic and that decay could not enter a closed sphere. Perhaps the Emperor wanted to re-create the beginning of time and called himself First in order to be really first. Perhaps he called himself Huang Ti in an endeavor to identify himself with that legendary Huang Ti, the emperor who invented writing and the compass and who, according to the Book of Rites, gave things their true names; for Shih Huang Ti boasted, on inscriptions that still exist, that all things under his reign had the names that befitted them. He dreamed of founding an immortal dynasty; he decreed that his heirs should be called Second Emperor, Third Emperor, Fourth Emperor, and so on to infinity.

I have spoken of a magic plan; we might also suppose that building the wall and burning the books were not simultaneous acts. And so, depending on the order we chose, we should have the image of a

4

king who began by destroying and then resigned himself to conserving; or the image of a disillusioned king who destroyed what he had previously defended. Both conjectures are dramatic; but as far as I know there is no historical truth in either. Herbert Allen Giles relates that anyone who concealed books was branded with a hot iron and condemned to work on the mammoth wall until the day of his death. That favors or tolerates another interpretation. Perhaps the wall was a metaphor; perhaps Shih Huang Ti condemned those who adored the past to a work as vast as the past, as stupid and as useless. Perhaps the wall was a kind of challenge and Shih Huang Ti thought, "Men love the past and I am powerless against that love, and so are my executioners; but some day there will be a man who feels as I do, and he will destroy the wall, as I have destroyed the books, and he will erase my memory and will be my shadow and my mirror and will not know it." Perhaps Shih Huang Ti walled his empire because he knew that it was fragile, and destroyed the books because he knew that they were sacred books (another name for books that teach what the whole universe or each man's conscience teaches). Perhaps the burning of the libraries and the building of the wall are operations that secretly nullify each other.

The tenacious wall, which at this moment, and always, projects its system of shadows over lands I shall never see, is the shadow of a Caesar who ordered the most reverent of nations to burn its past; and that idea—apart from the many conjectures it permits—is probably what we find so touching. (Its principal virtue may be in the contrast between construction and destruction on an enormous scale.) We could generalize, and infer that *all* forms possess virtue in themselves and not in a conjectural "content." That would support the theory of Benedetto Croce; in 1877 Pater had already stated that all the arts aspire to resemble music, which is pure form. Music, states of happiness, mythology, faces molded by time, certain twilights and certain places—all these are trying to tell us something, or have told us something we should not have missed, or are about to tell us something; that imminence of a revelation that is not yet produced is, perhaps, the aesthetic reality.

Buenos Aires, 1950

Pascal's Sphere

 Perhaps universal history is the history of a few metaphors. I should like to sketch one chapter of that history.

Six centuries before the Christian era Xenophanes of Colophon, the rhapsodist, weary of the Homeric verses he recited from city to city, attacked the poets who attributed anthropomorphic traits to the gods; the substitute he proposed to the Greeks was a single God: an eternal sphere. In Plato's *Timaeus* we read that the sphere is the most perfect and most uniform shape, because all points on its surface are equidistant from the center. Olof Gigon (*Ursprung der griechischen Philosophie*, 183) says that Xenophanes shared that belief; the God was spheroid, because that form was the best, or the least bad, to serve as a representation of the divinity. Forty years later, Parmenides of Elea repeated the image ("Being is like the mass of a well-rounded sphere, whose force is constant from the center in any direction"). Calogero and Mondolfo believe that he envisioned an infinite, or infinitely growing sphere, and that those words have a dynamic meaning (Albertelli, *Gli Eleati*, 148). Parmenides taught in Italy; a few years after he died, the Sicilian Empedocles of Agrigentum plotted a laborious cosmogony, in one section of which the particles of earth, air, fire, and water compose an endless sphere, "the round *Sphairos*, which rejoices in its circular solitude."

6

Universal history followed its course. The too-human gods attacked by Xenophanes were reduced to poetic fictions or to demons, but it was said that one god, Hermes Trismegistus, had dictated a variously estimated number of books (42, according to Clement of Alexandria; 20,000, according to Iamblichus; 36,525, according to the priests of Thoth, who is also Hermes), on whose pages all things were written. Fragments of that illusory library, compiled or forged since the third century, form the so-called *Hermetica*. In one part of the *Asclepius*, which was also attributed to Trismegistus, the twelfth-century French theologian, Alain de Lille—Alanus de Insulis—discovered this formula, which future generations would not forget: "God is an intelligible sphere, whose center is everywhere and whose circumference is nowhere." The Pre-Socratics spoke of an endless sphere; Albertelli (like Aristotle before him) thinks that such a statement is a *contradictio in adjecto*, because the subject and predicate negate each other. Possibly so, but the formula of the Hermetic books almost enables us to envisage that sphere. In the thirteenth century the image reappeared in the symbolic *Roman de la Rose*, which attributed it to Plato, and in the *Speculum Triplex* encyclopedia. In the sixteenth century the last chapter of the last book of *Pantagruel* referred to "that intellectual sphere, whose center is everywhere and whose circumference nowhere, which we call God." For the medieval mind, the meaning was clear: God is in each one of his creatures, but is not limited by any one of them. "Behold, the heaven and heaven of heavens cannot contain thee," said Solomon (I Kings 8:27). The geometrical metaphor of the sphere must have seemed like a gloss of those words.

Dante's poem has preserved Ptolemaic astronomy, which ruled men's imaginations for fourteen hundred years. The earth is the center of the universe. It is an immovable sphere, around which nine concentric spheres revolve. The first seven are the planetary heavens (the heavens of the Moon, Mercury, Venus, the Sun, Mars, Jupiter, and Saturn); the eighth, the Heaven of Fixed Stars; the ninth, the Crystalline Heaven (called the Primum Mobile), surrounded by the Empyrean, which is made of light. That whole laborious array of hollow, transparent, and revolving spheres (one system required fifty-five) had come to be a mental necessity. *De hypothesibus mo-*

7

tuum coelestium commentariolus was the timid title that Copernicus, the disputer of Aristotle, gave to the manuscript that transformed our vision of the cosmos. For one man, Giordano Bruno, the breaking of the sidereal vaults was a liberation. In *La cena de le ceneri* he proclaimed that the world was the infinite effect of an infinite cause and that the divinity was near, "because it is in us even more than we ourselves are in us." He searched for the words that would explain Copernican space to mankind, and on one famous page he wrote: "We can state with certainty that the universe is all center, or that the center of the universe is everywhere and the circumference nowhere" (*De la causa, principio e uno*, V).

That was written exultantly in 1584, still in the light of the Renaissance; seventy years later not one spark of that fervor remained and men felt lost in time and space. In time, because if the future and the past are infinite, there will not really be a when; in space, because if every being is equidistant from the infinite and the infinitesimal, there will not be a where. No one exists on a certain day, in a certain place; no one knows the size of his face. In the Renaissance humanity thought it had reached adulthood, and it said as much through the mouths of Bruno, Campanella, and Bacon. In the seventeenth century humanity was intimidated by a feeling of old age; to vindicate itself it exhumed the belief of a slow and fatal degeneration of all creatures because of Adam's sin. (In Genesis 5:27 we read that "all the days of Methuselah were nine hundred sixty and nine years"; in 6:4, that "There were giants in the earth in those days.") The elegy *Anatomy of the World*, by John Donne, deplored the very brief lives and the slight stature of contemporary men, who could be likened to fairies and dwarfs. According to Johnson's biography, Milton feared that an epic genre had become impossible on earth. Glanvill thought that Adam, God's medal, enjoyed a telescopic and microscopic vision. Robert South wrote, in famous words, that an Aristotle was merely the wreckage of Adam, and Athens, the rudiments of Paradise. In that jaded century the absolute space that inspired the hexameters of Lucretius, the absolute space that had been a liberation for Bruno, was a labyrinth and an abyss for Pascal. He hated the universe, and yearned to adore God. But God was less real to him than the hated universe. He was sorry that the firmament could not speak; he com-

8

pared our lives to those of shipwrecked men on a desert island. He felt the incessant weight of the physical world; he felt confused, afraid, and alone; and he expressed his feelings like this: "It [nature] is an infinite sphere, the center of which is everywhere, the circumference nowhere." That is the text of the Brunschvicg edition, but the critical edition of Tourneur (Paris, 1941), which reproduces the cancellations and the hesitations of the manuscript, reveals that Pascal started to write *effroyable:* "A frightful sphere, the center of which is everywhere, and the circumference nowhere."

Perhaps universal history is the history of the diverse intonation of a few metaphors.

Buenos Aires, 1951

The Flower of Coleridge

Around 1938 Paul Valéry wrote that the history of literature should not be the history of the authors and the accidents of their careers or of the career of their works, but rather the history of the Spirit as the producer or consumer of literature. He added that such a history could be written without the mention of a single writer. It was not the first time that the Spirit had made such an observation. In 1844 one of its amanuenses in Concord had noted: "I am very much struck in literature by the appearance that one person wrote all the books; . . . there is such equality and identity both of judgment and point of view in the narrative that it is plainly the work of one all-seeing, all-hearing gentleman" (Emerson, *Essays: Second Series*, "Nominalist and Realist," 1844). Twenty years earlier Shelley expressed the opinion that all the poems of the past, present, and future were episodes or fragments of a single infinite poem, written by all the poets on earth.

Those considerations (which are, of course, implicit in pantheism) could give rise to an endless debate. I am invoking them now to assist me in a modest plan: to trace the history of the evolution of an idea through the heterogeneous texts of three authors. The first one is by Coleridge; I am not sure whether he wrote it at the end of the eighteenth century or at the beginning of the nineteenth: "If a man

10

could pass through Paradise in a dream, and have a flower presented to him as a pledge that his soul had really been there, and if he found that flower in his hand when he awoke—Ay!—and what then?"

I wonder what my reader thinks of that imagining. To me it is perfect. It seems quite impossible to use it as the basis of other inventions, for it has the integrity and the unity of a *terminus ad quem*, a final goal. And of course it is just that; in the sphere of literature as in others, every act is the culmination of an infinite series of causes and the cause of an infinite series of effects. Behind Coleridge's idea is the general and ancient idea of the generations of lovers who begged for a flower as a token.

The second text I shall quote is a novel that Wells drafted in 1887 and rewrote seven years later, in the summer of 1894. The first version was entitled *The Chronic Argonauts* (here *chronic* was the etymological equivalent of *temporal*); the definitive version of the work was called *The Time Machine*. In that novel Wells continued and renewed a very ancient literary tradition: the foreseeing of future events. Isaiah *sees* the destruction of Babylon and the restoration of Israel; Aeneas, the military destiny of his descendants, the Romans; the prophet of the *Edda Saemundi*, the return of the gods who, after the cyclical battle in which our world will be destroyed, will discover that the same chess pieces they were playing with before are lying on the grass of a new meadow. Unlike those prophetic spectators, Wells's protagonist travels physically to the future. He returns tired, dusty, and shaken from a remote humanity that has divided into species who hate each other (the idle *eloi*, who live in dilapidated palaces and ruinous gardens; the subterranean and nyctalopic *morlocks* who feed on the *eloi*). He returns with his hair grown gray and brings with him a wilted flower from the future. This is the second version of Coleridge's image. More incredible than a celestial flower or the flower of a dream is the flower of the future, the unlikely flower whose atoms now occupy other spaces and have not yet been assembled.

The third version I shall mention, the most improbable of all, is the invention of a much more complex writer than Wells, although he was less gifted with those pleasant virtues that are usually called classical. I am referring to the author of *The Abasement of the Northmores*, the sad and labyrinthine Henry James. When he died, he left

11

the unfinished novel *The Sense of the Past*, an imaginative work which was a variation or elaboration of *The Time Machine*.[1] Wells's protagonist travels to the future in an outlandish vehicle that advances or recedes in time as other vehicles do in space; James's protagonist returns to the past, to the eighteenth century, by identifying himself with that period. (Both procedures are impossible, but James's is less arbitrary.) In *The Sense of the Past* the nexus between the real and the imaginative (between present and past) is not a flower, as in the previous stories, but a picture from the eighteenth century that mysteriously represents the protagonist. Fascinated by this canvas, he succeeds in going back to the day when it was painted. He meets a number of persons, including the artist, who paints him with fear and aversion, because he senses that there is something unusual and anomalous in those future features. James thus creates an incomparable *regressus in infinitum*, when his hero Ralph Pendrel returns to the eighteenth century because he is fascinated by an old painting, but Pendrel's return to this century is a condition for the existence of the painting. The cause follows the effect, the reason for the journey is one of the consequences of the journey.

Quite probably Wells was not acquainted with Coleridge's text; Henry James knew and admired the text of Wells. If the doctrine that all authors are one is valid, such facts are insignificant.[2] Strictly speaking, it is not necessary to go that far; the pantheist who declares that the plurality of authors is illusory finds unexpected support in the classicist, to whom that plurality matters but little. For classical minds the literature is the essential thing, not the individuals. George Moore and James Joyce have incorporated in their works the pages and sentences of others; Oscar Wilde used to give plots away for others to develop; both procedures, although they appear to be contradictory, may reveal an identical artistic perception—an ecumeni-

---

[1] I have not read *The Sense of the Past*, but I am acquainted with the competent analysis of it by Stephen Spender in his book *The Destructive Element* (pp. 105–110). James was a friend of Wells; to learn more about their relationship, consult the latter's vast *Experiment in Autobiography*.

[2] About the middle of the seventeenth century the epigrammatist of pantheism, Angelus Silesius, said that all the blessed are one (*Cherubinischer Wandersmann*, V, 7) and that every Christian must be Christ (*ibid.*, V, 9).

cal, impersonal perception. Another witness of the profound unity of the Word, another who denied the limitations of the individual, was the renowned Ben Jonson, who, when writing his literary testament and the favorable or adverse opinions he held of his contemporaries, was obliged to combine fragments from Seneca, Quintilian, Justus Lipsius, Vives, Erasmus, Machiavelli, Bacon, and the two Scaligers.

One last observation. Those who carefully copy a writer do it impersonally, do it because they confuse that writer with literature, do it because they suspect that to leave him at any one point is to deviate from reason and orthodoxy. For many years I thought that the almost infinite world of literature was in one man. That man was Carlyle, he was Johannes Becher, he was Whitman, he was Rafael Cansinos-Assens, he was De Quincey.

The Dream of Coleridge

The lyrical fragment "Kubla Khan" (fifty-odd rhymed and ir-regular verses of exquisite prosody) was dreamed by the English poet Samuel Taylor Coleridge on a summer day in 1797. Coleridge writes that he had retired to a farm near Exmoor; an indis-position obliged him to take a sedative; sleep overcame him a few moments after he had read a passage from Purchas describing the construction of a palace by Kubla Khan, the emperor who was made famous in the West by Marco Polo. In the dream the lines that had been read casually germinated and grew; the sleeping man perceived by intuition a series of visual images and, simultaneously, the words that expressed them. After a few hours he awoke with the certainty that he had composed, or received, a poem of about three hundred verses. He remembered them with singular clarity and was able to write down the fragment that is now part of his work. An unexpected visitor interrupted him and afterward he was unable to remember any more. To his no small surprise and mortification, although he still retained "some vague and dim recollection of the general purport of the vision, yet, with the exception of some eight or ten scattered lines and images, all the rest had passed away like the images on the surface of a stream into which a stone has been cast, but, alas! without the after restoration of the latter!" Coleridge wrote.

Swinburne felt that what he had been able to salvage was the su-

14

preme example of music in the English language, and that to try to analyze it would be like trying to unravel a rainbow (the metaphor belongs to John Keats). Summaries or descriptions of poetry whose principal virtue is music are useless and would only defeat our purpose; so then let us merely remember that Coleridge was given a page of undisputed splendor *in a dream.*

Although the case is quite extraordinary, it is not unique. In the psychological study *The World of Dreams* Havelock Ellis has compared it to the case of the violinist and composer, Giuseppe Tartini, who dreamed that the Devil (his slave) was playing a prodigious sonata on the violin; when the dreamer awoke he played *Trillo del Diavolo* from memory. Another classic example of unconscious cerebration is that of Robert Louis Stevenson; as he himself has related in his "Chapter on Dreams," one dream gave him the plot of *Olalla* and another, in 1884, the plot of *Jekyll and Hyde.* Tartini undertook to imitate the music he had heard in a dream. Stevenson received outlines of plots from his dreams. More akin to Coleridge's verbal inspiration is the inspiration attributed by the Venerable Bede to Caedmon (*Historia ecclesiastica gentis Anglorum,* IV, 24). The case occurred at the end of the seventh century in the missionary and warring England of the Saxon kingdoms. Caedmon was an uneducated herdsman and was no longer young; one night he slipped away from a festive gathering because he knew that they would pass the harp to him and he knew also that he could not sing. He fell asleep in the stable near the horses, and in a dream someone called him by name and told him to sing. Caedmon replied that he did not know how to sing, but the voice said, "Sing about the origin of created things." Then Caedmon recited verses he had never heard before. He did not forget them when he awoke, and was able to repeat them to the monks at the nearby monastery of Hild. Although he did not know how to read, the monks explained passages of sacred history to him and he ruminated on them like a clean animal and converted them into delightful verses. He sang about the creation of the world and man and the story of Genesis; the Exodus of the children of Israel and their entrance into the Promised Land; the Incarnation, Passion, Resurrection, and Ascension of the Lord; the coming of the Holy Spirit; the teaching of the Apostles; and also the terror of the Last Judgment, the horror of Infernal Punishments, the delights of Heaven, and the graces and punishments of God. He was the first sacred poet of the English nation. Bede wrote that no one equaled him because he did not learn from men, but from God. Years later he foretold the hour of his death and awaited it in sleep. Let us hope that he met his angel again.

At first glance the dream of Coleridge may appear to be less astonishing than his precursor's. "Kubla Khan" is an admirable composition, and the principal merit of the nine-line hymn dreamed by Caedmon is that its origin was in a dream; but Coleridge was already a poet while Caedmon's vocation was revealed to him. Nevertheless, a later event makes the marvel of the dream in which "Kubla Khan" was engendered even more mysterious. If it is true, the story of Coleridge's dream began many centuries before Coleridge and has not yet ended.

The poet's dream occurred in 1797 (some say 1798), and he published his account of the dream in 1816 as a gloss or a justification of the unfinished poem. Twenty years later the first western version of one of those universal histories that are so abundant in Persian literature appeared in Paris, in fragmentary form—the *General History of the World* by Rashid al-Din, which dates from the fourteenth century. One line reads as follows: "East of Shang-tu, Kubla Khan built a palace according to a plan that he had seen in a dream and retained in his memory." Rashid al-Din was the Vizir of Ghazan Mahmud, a descendant of Kubla.

A thirteenth-century Mongolian emperor dreams a palace and then builds it according to his dream; an eighteenth-century English poet (who could not have known that the structure was derived from a dream) dreams a poem about the palace. In comparison with this symmetry, which operates on the souls of sleeping men and spans continents and centuries, the levitations, resurrections, and apparitions in the sacred books are not so extraordinary.

But how shall we explain it? Those who automatically reject the supernatural (I try, always, to belong to this group) will claim that the story of the two dreams is merely a coincidence, a chance delineation, like the outlines of lions or horses we sometimes see in clouds. Others will argue that the poet somehow found out that the Emperor

16

had dreamed the palace, and then said he had dreamed the poem in order to create a splendid fiction that would also palliate or justify the truncated and rhapsodic quality of the verses.[1] That conjecture seems reasonable, but it obliges us to postulate, arbitrarily, a text not identified by Sinologists in which Coleridge was able to read, before 1816, about Kubla's dream.[2] Hypotheses that transcend reason are more appealing. One such theory is that the Emperor's soul penetrated Coleridge's, enabling Coleridge to rebuild the destroyed palace in words that would be more lasting than marble and metal.

The first dream added a palace to reality; the second, which occurred five centuries later, a poem (or the beginning of a poem) suggested by the palace. The similarity of the dreams reveals a plan; the enormous length of time involved reveals a superhuman performer. To inquire the purpose of that immortal or long-lived being would perhaps be as foolhardy as futile, but it seems likely that he has not yet achieved it. In 1691 Father Gerbillon of the Society of Jesus confirmed that ruins were all that was left of the palace of Kubla Khan; we know that scarcely fifty lines of the poem were salvaged. Those facts give rise to the conjecture that the series of dreams and labors has not yet ended. The first dreamer was given the vision of the palace and he built it; the second, who did not know of the other's dream, was given the poem about the palace. If the plan does not fail, some reader of "Kubla Khan" will dream, on a night centuries removed from us, of marble or of music. This man will not know that two others also dreamed. Perhaps the series of dreams has no end, or perhaps the last one who dreams will have the key.

After writing all this, I perceive—or think that I perceive—another explanation. Perhaps an archetype not yet revealed to men, an eternal object (to use Whitehead's term), is gradually entering the world; its first manifestation was the palace; its second was the poem. Whoever compared them would have seen that they were essentially the same.

---

[1] At the beginning of the nineteenth century or at the end of the eighteenth, judged by readers of classical taste, "Kubla Khan" was much more outrageous than it is now. In 1884 Coleridge's first biographer, Traill, could still write: "The extravagant dream poem 'Kubla Khan' is little more than a psychological curiosity."

[2] See John Livingston Lowes, *The Road to Xanadu* (1927), pp. 358, 585.

Time and J. W. Dunne

In Number 63 of *Sur* (December, 1939) I published a prehistory, a first basic history, of infinite regression. Not all my omissions were involuntary: I deliberately excluded the mention of J. W. Dunne, who has derived from the interminable *regressus* a rather surprising doctrine on time and the observer. The discussion (the mere exposition) of his thesis would have exceeded the limitations of my essay. Its complexity required a separate article, and I shall attempt it now, after having perused Dunne's latest book, *Nothing Dies* (1940), which repeats or summarizes the plots of his three earlier works.

Or rather, the plot. There is nothing new in its mechanism; but the author's inferences are most unusual, almost scandalous. Before commenting on them, I shall mention some earlier manifestations of the premises.

The seventh of the many philosophical systems of India recorded by Paul Deussen (*Nachvedische Philosophie der Inder*, 318) denies that the self can be an immediate object of knowledge, "because if our soul were knowable, a second soul would be required to know the first and a third to know the second." The Hindus have no historical sense (that is, they stubbornly prefer to examine ideas rather than the names and dates of philosophers); but we know that this radical negation of introspection is about eight centuries old. Schopenhauer

18

rediscovers it around 1843. "The knower himself," he repeats, "cannot be known precisely as such, otherwise he would be the known of another knower" (*Welt als Wille und Vorstellung*, II, 19). Herbart also played with that kind of ontological multiplication. Before he was twenty he had reasoned that the self must be infinite, since the fact of one's knowing oneself postulates another self which also knows itself, and that self in turn postulates another self (Deussen, *Die neuere Philosophie*, 1920, p. 367). Dunne uses this plot, embellishing it with anecdotes, parables, strokes of irony, and diagrams.

Dunne (*An Experiment with Time*, Chapter XXII) reasons that a conscious subject is conscious not only of what it observes, but of a subject A that also observes and, therefore, of another subject B that is conscious of A and, therefore, of another subject C conscious of B. He adds mysteriously that those innumerable intimate observers do not fit into the three dimensions of space, but can and do exist in the multitudinous dimensions of time. Before clarifying that clarification, I invite my readers to join me in thinking about the meaning of this paragraph again.

Huxley, the heir of the British nominalists, maintains that only a verbal difference exists between the act of perceiving a pain and the act of knowing that one perceives it, and he derides the pure metaphysicians who distinguish in every sensation a sensible subject, a sensation-producing object and that imperious personage: the Ego (*Essays*, Vol. VI, p. 87). Gustav Spiller (*The Mind of Man*, 1902) concedes that the awareness of pain and pain itself are two different things, but he considers them to be as comprehensible as the simultaneous perception of a voice and a face. I believe his opinion is valid. As to the consciousness of consciousness that Dunne invokes to establish in each individual a bewildering and nebulous hierarchy of subjects, or observers, I prefer to suspect that they are successive (or imaginary) states of the initial subject. Leibnitz has said, "If the spirit had to reflect on each thought, the mere perception of a sensation would cause it to think of the sensation and then to think of the thought and then of the thought of the thought, and so to infinity" (*Nouveaux essais sur l'entendement humain*, Bk. II, Chap. I).

Dunne's procedure for the immediate attainment of an infinite number of times is less convincing and more ingenious. Like Juan de

19

Mena in his *El laberinto de Fortuna*,[1] like Uspenski in the *Tertium Organum*, he states that the future already exists, with its vicissitudes and its details. Toward the pre-existent future (or from the pre-existent future, as Bradley prefers) flows the absolute river of cosmic time, or the mortal rivers of our lives. That movement, that flowing requires a definite length of time, like all movement; we shall have a second time for the movement of the first; a third for the movement of the second, and so on to infinity.[2] That is the system proposed by Dunne. In those hypothetical or illusory times the imperceptible subjects multiplied by the other *regressus* have an interminable dwelling place.

I wonder what my reader may think of this. I don't pretend to know what sort of thing time is—or even if it is a "thing"—but I feel that the passage of time and time itself are a single mystery and not two. Dunne, I suspect, makes a mistake like the one made by the addled poets who speak of, say, the moon which reveals its red disk, thus substituting a subject, a verb and an object for an undivided visual image; because the object is merely the subject itself, flimsily disguised. Dunne is a famous victim of that bad intellectual habit denounced by Bergson: to conceive of time as a fourth dimension of space. He postulates that the future already exists and that we must move to it, but that postulate suffices to convert it into space and to require a second time (which is also conceived in spatial form, in the form of a line or a river) and then a third and a millionth. Not one of Dunne's four books fails to propose infinite dimensions of time,[3] but those dimensions are spatial. For Dunne, real time is the unattainable final boundary of an infinite series.

---

[1] In this fifteenth-century poem there is a vision of "three great wheels": the first, motionless, is the past; the second, in motion, is the present; the third, motionless, is the future.

[2] A half century before Dunne proposed it, "the absurd conjecture of a second time, in which the first flows rapidly or slowly," was discovered and rejected by Schopenhauer, in a handwritten note added to his *Welt als Wille und Vorstellung* which is recorded on p. 829 of Vol. II of the historico-critical edition by Otto Weiss.

[3] The phrase is revealing. In Chapter XXI of *An Experiment with Time* he speaks of one time that is perpendicular to another.

What reasons are there for assuming that the future already exists? Dunne gives two: one, premonitory dreams; another, the relative simplicity that this hypothesis gives to the inextricable diagrams that are typical of his style. He also wishes to elude the problems of a continuous creation.

Theologians define eternity as the simultaneous and lucid possession of all instants of time and declare it to be one of the divine attributes. Dunne, surprisingly, supposes that eternity is already ours and that the dreams we have each night corroborate this. According to him, the immediate past and the immediate future flow together in our dreams. While we are awake we pass through successive time at a uniform speed; in dreams we span an area that may be very vast. To dream is to coordinate the objects we viewed while awake and to weave a story, or a series of stories, out of them. We see the image of a sphinx and the image of a drugstore, and then we invent a drugstore that is changed into a sphinx. We put the mouth of a face that looked at us the night before last on the man we shall meet tomorrow. (Schopenhauer wrote that life and dreams were pages from the same book, and that to read them in their proper order was to live, but to scan them at random was to dream.)

Dunne assures us that in death we shall learn how to handle eternity successfully. We shall recover all the moments of our lives and we shall combine them as we please. God and our friends and Shakespeare will collaborate with us.

With such a splendid thesis as that, any fallacy committed by the author becomes insignificant.

The Creation and P. H. Gosse

"The man without a Navel yet lives in me" is the curious line written by Sir Thomas Browne (*Religio Medici*, 1642) to signify that he was conceived in sin because he was a descendant of Adam. In the first chapter of *Ulysses*, Joyce also evokes the immaculate and taut belly of the woman without a mother: "Heva, naked Eve. She had no navel." The subject (I know) can easily become grotesque and trivial, but the zoologist Philip Henry Gosse has connected it to the central problem of metaphysics: the problem of time. That connection dates from the year 1857; eighty years of oblivion are perhaps equal to novelty.

In two different parts of the Bible (Romans 5; I Corinthians 15) the first Adam, in whom all die, is compared to the last Adam, who is Jesus.[1] If the comparison is not to be a mere blasphemy, it must

---

[1] In religious poetry this association is common. Perhaps the most intense example is in the penultimate stanza of the "Hymn to God, my God, in my sickness," March 23, 1630, by John Donne:

> We think that Paradise and Calvary,
> Christ's Cross, and Adam's tree, stood in one place,
> Look Lord, and find both Adams met in me;
> As the first Adam's sweat surrounds my face,
> May the last Adam's blood my soul embrace.

presuppose a certain enigmatic parity, which is translated into myths and symmetries. The *Legenda aurea* relates that the wood of the Cross comes from the forbidden Tree of Paradise; theologians say that Adam's age at the time he was created by the Father was the precise age at which the Son died: thirty-three. This senseless precision must have had an influence on the cosmogony of Gosse.

He revealed it in the book *Omphalos* (London, 1857), subtitled *An Attempt to Untie the Geological Knot.* Since I was unable to find the book in any library, I shall refer to the summaries made by Edmund Gosse (*Father and Son*, 1907) and H. G. Wells (*All Aboard for Ararat*, 1940). The illustrations I shall use do not appear on those brief pages, but I feel they are compatible with the thought of Gosse.

In the chapter of *Logic* that considers the law of causality, John Stuart Mill affirms that the state of the universe at any instant is a consequence of its state at the previous instant and that for an infinite intelligence the perfect knowledge of a *single instant* would make it possible to know the history of the universe, both past and future. (He says also—oh Louis Auguste Blanqui, oh Nietzsche, oh Pythagoras!—that the repetition of any one state of the universe would bring about the repetition of all the others and would make universal history a cyclical series.) In that tempered version of one of Laplace's fantasies—Laplace had imagined that the present state of the universe, in theory, could be reduced to a formula from which Someone would be able to deduce the whole future and the whole past—Mill does not exclude the possibility that a future exterior intervention may break the series. He asserts that state q will inevitably produce state r; state r, s; state s, t; but he concedes that before t a divine catastrophe—the *consummatio mundi*, say—may have annihilated the planet. The future is inexorable, precise, but it may not happen. God lies in wait in the intervals.

In 1857 men were perturbed by a conflict. Genesis attributed six days—six unequivocal Hebrew days, from sunset to sunset—to the divine creation of the world; the impious paleontologists insisted on enormous accumulations of time for the same result. De Quincey repeated it in vain: the Bible has an obligation not to instruct men in any science, since sciences constitute a vast mechanism to develop and train the human intellect. How can one reconcile God with the fossils, or Sir Charles Lyell with Moses? Gosse, fortified by prayer, proposed an astonishing answer.

Mill imagines a causal, infinite time that may be interrupted by a future act of God, while Gosse imagines a rigorously causal, infinite time that has been interrupted by a past act: the Creation. State n will inevitably produce state v, but before v the Universal Judgment may occur; state n presupposes state c, but state c has not occurred, because the world was created at f or h. The first instant of time coincides with the instant of the Creation, as St. Augustine says; that first instant tolerates not only an infinite future, but an infinite past. A past that is hypothetical, to be sure, but also precise and inevitable. Adam appears and his teeth and his skeleton are those of a man of thirty-three; Adam appears (writes Edmund Gosse) and he has a navel, although no umbilical cord attached him to a mother. The principle of reason requires that no result be without a cause, and those causes require other causes, which are multiplied regressively;[2] there are concrete vestiges of them all, but only those that are posterior to the Creation have really existed. There are glyptodont skeletons in the gorge of Luján, but glyptodonts never existed. That is the ingenious (and, above all, incredible) thesis that Philip Henry Gosse proposed to religion and to science.

But both rejected it. To newspaper reporters it became simply the doctrine that God had hidden fossils underground to test the faith of geologists; Charles Kingsley denied that the Lord had carved a superfluous and vast lie on the rocks. In vain Gosse explained the metaphysical core of his thesis: that one instant of time was inconceivable without another instant before it and another after it and so on to infinity. I wonder if he knew the ancient sentence that is quoted at the beginning of the Talmudic anthology by Rafael Cansinos-Assens: "It was only the first night, but a number of centuries had already preceded it."

I should like to emphasize two virtues in Gosse's forgotten thesis. First: its rather monstrous elegance. Second: its involuntary reduction of a *creatio ex nihilo* to absurdity, its indirect demonstration

2 Cf. Spencer, *Facts and Comments* (1902), pp. 148–151.

that the universe is eternal, as the Vedanta, Heraclitus, Spinoza, and the atomists thought. Bertrand Russell has brought the thesis up to date. In the ninth chapter of *The Analysis of Mind* (London, 1921) he theorizes that the planet was created a few minutes ago, with a humanity that "remembers" an illusory past.

Buenos Aires, 1941

Postscript: In 1802 Chateaubriand (*Génie du christianisme*, I, 4, 5) with aesthetic reasons as his point of departure, formulated a thesis exactly like Gosse's. He denounced as banal and ridiculous a first day of the Creation, populated by young pigeons, larvae, puppies and seeds. "Sans une vieillesse originaire, la nature dans son innocence eût été moins belle qu'elle ne l'est aujourd'hui dans sa corruption," he wrote.

Dr. Américo Castro Is Alarmed

The word *problem* may be an insidious *petitio principii*. To speak of the *Jewish problem* is to postulate that the Jews are a problem; it is to predict (and recommend) persecution, plunder, shooting, beheading, rape, and the reading of Dr. Rosenberg's prose. Another disadvantage of fallacious problems is that they bring about solutions that are equally fallacious. Pliny (Book VIII of *Natural History*) is not satisfied with the observation that dragons attack elephants in the summer; he ventures the hypothesis that they do it in order to drink the elephants' blood, which, as everyone knows, is very cold. Dr. Castro (*La peculiaridad lingüística rioplatense y su sentido histórico* [Losada, Buenos Aires, 1941] is not content to observe that there is a "linguistic disorder in Buenos Aires": he ventures the hypothesis of "slangism" and "gauchophile mystique."

To demonstrate the first thesis—the corruption of the Spanish language in the River Plate area—the doctor employs a method that we must classify as sophistic, to avoid casting aspersions on his intelligence; as ingenuous, to banish doubts regarding his integrity. He collects bits and pieces from Pacheco, Vacarezza, Lima, *Last Reason*, Contursi, Enrique González Tuñón, Palermo, Llanderas, and Malfatti; he copies them with childlike seriousness and then exhibits them *urbi et orbi* as examples of our depraved language. He does not suspect that these exercises (*"Con un feca con chele / y una*

26

ensaimada / vos te venís pal Centro / de gran bacán") are merely caricatures; he declares that they are "symptoms of a grave disorder," caused by "the well-known circumstances that made the River Plate an area where the heartbeat of the Spanish Empire had lost much of its vigor." One could argue just as effectively that there are no traces of Spanish left in Madrid, using as proof the following couplets quoted by Rafael Salillas in his book, *El delincuente español: su lenguaje* (1896):

> El minche de esa rumi
> dicen no tenela bales;
> los he dicaito yo,
> los tenela muy juncales . . .

> El chibel barba del breje
> menjindé a los burós:
> apincharé ararajay
> y menda la pirabó.

After such an example of unmitigated obscurity this miserable couplet in Argentine slang is almost limpid:

> El bacán le acanaló
> el escracho a la minushia;
> después espirajushió
> por temor a la canushia.[1]

On page 139 Dr. Castro mentions another book about the linguistic problem in Buenos Aires; on page 87 he boasts of having deciphered a rustic dialogue by Lynch "in which the characters use the most barbarous means of expression; only those of us who are familiar with River Plate jargons can understand them completely." Jargons: *ce pluriel est bien singulier.* Except for Argentine slang (a modest dialect that no one dreams of comparing to the exuberant

---

[1] This is included in the dictionary of jargon by Luis Villamayor, *The Language of the Populace; El lenguaje del bajo fondo* (Buenos Aires, 1915). Castro is not acquainted with this dictionary, perhaps because it is mentioned by Arturo Costa Alvarez in a key work, *Argentine Spanish; El castellano en la Argentina* (La Plata, 1928). Needless to say, no one says *minushia, canushia, espirajushiar.*

caló of the Spaniards), there are no jargons in this country. We do not suffer from dialects, although we do indeed suffer from dialectological institutes. Those organizations thrive on condemning each successive slang they invent. They have improvised *gauchesco*, based on Hernández; *cocoliche*, derived from a clown who worked with the Podestá brothers; *vesre*, taken from fourth-grade students. They have phonographs; before long they will record *Catita's* voice. They are dependent on such rubbish; we owe and shall continue to owe those dubious riches to them.

No less fallacious are "the serious problems of the spoken language in Buenos Aires." I have traveled through Catalonia, Alicante, Andalusia, Castile; I have lived in Valldemosa for two years and in Madrid for one; I have very fond memories of those places, but I never noticed that Spaniards spoke better than we did. (True, they speak *louder*, with the aplomb of those who know no doubt.) Dr. Castro accuses us of archaism. His method is curious: he discovers that the most cultivated persons in San Mamed de Puga, Orense, have forgotten a certain usage of a certain word; he immediately decides that the Argentines should forget it, too. The fact is that the Spanish language suffers from various imperfections (a monotonous prevalence of vowels, excessive diversity of the words, inability to form compound words), but not the imperfection claimed by its inept defenders: difficulty. Spanish is very easy. Only Spaniards do not believe that: perhaps because they are dazzled by the charms of Catalán, Bable, Mallorcan, Galician, Basque, or Valencian; perhaps because of an error of vanity; perhaps because of a certain verbal crudity (they confuse the accusative and the dative, they say *le mató* for *lo mató*, they are usually incapable of pronouncing *Atlántico* or *Madrid*, they think that a book can bear this cacophonous title: *La peculiaridad lingüística rioplatense y su sentido histórico*).

On every page Dr. Castro abounds in conventional superstitions. He scorns López and venerates Ricardo Rojas; he repudiates the tango and makes respectful allusions to the *jácara*; he thinks that Rosas was a leader of insurgents, a man like Ramírez or Artigas, and gives him the ridiculous name *maximum centaur*. (With better style and more lucid judgment Groussac preferred the definition "rearguard militiaman.") He proscribes—and I believe rightly—the word

28

cachada, but he accepts *tomadura de pelo*, which is not noticeably more logical or more charming. He attacks Latin American idiocies because he likes Spanish idiocies better. He does not want us to say *de arriba*; he wants us to say *de gorra*. This examiner of the "linguistic reality of Buenos Aires" says in all seriousness that the inhabitants of that city call lobster *acridio*; this inexplicable reader of Carlos de la Púa and *Yacaré* tells us that *taita*, in Argentine dialect, means "father."

The form of the book is no better than the content. At times the style becomes commercial: "The libraries of Mexico had books of high quality" (p. 49); "The customs . . . charged fabulous duties" (p. 52). Again, the continual triviality of the thought does not exclude the picturesque absurdity: "Then the only thing possible, the tyrant, appears; he is the condensation of the undirected energy of the masses, whom he does not lead because he is not a guide but rather a crushing force, a huge orthopedic apparatus that mechanically, bestially herds the disbanding flock" (pp. 71, 72). Sometimes the author attempts the *mot juste:* ". . . for the same reasons that caused the marvelous grammar of A. Alonso and P. Henríquez Ureña to be torpedoed" (p. 31).

Devotees of *Last Reason* compose equine metaphors; Dr. Castro, who is more versatile in his errors, unites radio and football:

The thought and the art of the River Plate region are valuable antennae for everything of worth and value; this intensely receptive attitude will soon become a creative force, if fate does not change the direction of the propitious signals. Poetry, the novel, and the essay have achieved more than one perfect goal there. Among the cultivators of science and of philosophical thinking in that area are names of the greatest distinction. (p. 9)

Dr. Castro adds the indefatigable practice of flattery, rhymed prose, and terrorism to his erroneous and minuscule erudition.

Postscript: On page 136 I read: "It is incredible that anyone seriously, without irony, would try to write like Ascasubi, del Campo, or Hernández."

I should like to quote the final stanzas of *Martín Fierro:*

Cruz y Fierro de una estancia
Una tropilla se arriaron,
Por delante se la echaron
Como criollos entendidos
Y pronto, sin ser sentidos,
Por la frontera cruzaron.

Y cuando la habían pasao
Una madrugada clara,
Le dijo Cruz que mirara
Las últimas poblaciones;
Y a Fierro dos lagrimones
Le rodaron por la cara.

Y siguiendo el fiel del rumbo,
Se entraron en el desierto,
No sé si los habrán muerto
En alguna correría
Pero espero que algún día
Sabré de ellos algo cierto.

Y ya con estas noticias
Mi relación acabé,
Por ser ciertas las conté,
Todas las desgracias dichas:
Es un telar de desdichas
Cada gaucho que usté vé.

Pero ponga su esperanza
En el Dios que lo formó,
Y aquí me despido yo
Que he relatao a mi modo,
Males que conocen todos
Pero que naides cantó.

"Seriously, without irony," I ask: Who is more dialectal: the poet whose limpid verses you have just read, or the incoherent man who writes about an orthopedic apparatus that herds a flock, literary genres that play football, and torpedoed grammars?

On page 122 Dr. Castro has enumerated several writers whose style is correct. In spite of the inclusion of my name on that list, I do not consider myself entirely unqualified to speak of stylistics.

A Note on Carriego

In these times we all see Evaristo Carriego in connection with the suburban locale, and we tend to forget that Carriego is (like the man about town, the little seamstress, and the foreigner) a creation of Carriego, just as the suburb in which we place him is a projection and almost an illusion of his work. Oscar Wilde thought that Japan—the images evoked by that word—had been invented by Hokusai; in the case of Evaristo Carriego, we must postulate a reciprocal action: the suburb creates Carriego and is re-created by him. Carriego is influenced by the real suburb and the suburb of Trejo and the *milongas*; Carriego imposes his vision of the suburb on us; and that vision changes reality. (Later, reality will be changed much more by the tango and the theatre.)

How did it happen, how could the unhappy boy Carriego become the man he will now be forever? Perhaps if he were asked, not even Carriego himself could tell us. Without any justification except my inability to imagine things differently, I suggest this version:

One day in 1904, in a house that is still standing on Honduras Street, Evaristo Carriego was rereading a book about the adventures of Charles de Baatz, Lord of Artagnan. He read it avidly, because Dumas offered him what Shakespeare or Balzac or Walt Whitman offers to others, a taste of the fullness of life; he read it sadly, because he was young, proud, timid, and poor, and he felt cut off from life.

Life was in France, he thought, when the steel blades flashed, or when the Emperor's armies overran the land, but here I am in the twentieth century, the too-late twentieth century, in an unimportant suburb of South America.

As Carriego was thinking those thoughts something happened. The persistent strumming of a guitar, the uneven row of low houses seen through the window, Juan Muraña tipping his hat to acknowledge a greeting (the same Juan Muraña who, the night before last, left his mark on the face of Suárez the Chilean), the moon seen in the square opening of the patio, an old man with a fighting cock, something, anything. Something we cannot recapture, something whose content but not form we know, something quotidian and trivial and previously unperceived which revealed to Carriego that the universe (which gives itself completely in each instant, in any place, and not only in the works of Dumas) was in the present too, in Palermo, Argentina, in 1904. "Enter, for the gods are here also," said Heraclitus of Ephesus to the people who found him warming himself at the kitchen stove.

I suspected once that any human life, however intricate and full it might be, consisted in reality of *one* moment: the moment when a man knows for all time who he is. From the moment of the unknown revelation I have attempted to re-create, Carriego is Carriego. He is already the author of the verses which, years later, he will be permitted to invent:

> Le cruzan el rostro, de estigmas violentos,
> Hondas cicatrices, y tal vez le halaga
> Llevar imborrables adornos sangrientos:
> Caprichos de hembra que tuvo la daga.

In the last line, almost miraculously, there is an echo of the medieval imagining about the marriage of the warrior to his sword, of the imagining that Detlev von Liliencron framed in other illustrious verses:

> In die Friesen trug er sein Schwert Hilfnot,
> das hat ihn heute betrogen . . .

Our Poor Individualism

The illusions of patriotism are limitless. In the first century of our era Plutarch ridiculed those who declared that the moon of Athens was better than the moon of Corinth; in the seventeenth century Milton observed that God usually revealed Himself first to His Englishmen; at the beginning of the nineteenth, Fichte declared that to have character and to be German were, obviously, the same thing. Here in Argentina, nationalists are much in evidence; they tell us they are motivated by the worthy or innocent desire to foment the best Argentine traits. But they do not really know the Argentine people; in speeches they prefer to define them in terms of some external fact—the Spanish *conquistadores*, say, or an imaginary Catholic tradition or "Saxon imperialism."

Unlike North Americans and almost all Europeans, the Argentine does not identify himself with the State. That can be explained by the fact that, in this country, the governments are usually exceedingly bad, or the State is an inconceivable abstraction;[1] the truth is that the Argentine is an individual, not a citizen. Aphorisms like Hegel's—"The State is the reality of the moral idea"—seem like a

---

[1] The State is impersonal; the Argentine can think only in terms of a personal relationship. Therefore, he does not consider stealing public funds a crime. I am simply stating a fact; I do not justify or condone it.

33

vicious joke. Films made in Hollywood repeatedly portray as admirable the man (generally a reporter) who tries to make friends with a criminal so he can turn him over to the police later; the Argentine, for whom friendship is a passion and the police something like a *maffia*, feels that this "hero" is an incomprehensible cad. He agrees with Don Quixote that "no one is without sin" and that "good men should not be the executioners of the others" (*Don Quixote*, I, XXII). More than once, as I confronted the vain symmetries of Spanish style, I have suspected that we differ irrevocably from Spain; but those two lines from the *Quixote* have sufficed to convince me of my error; they are like the calm and secret symbol of our affinity. One night of Argentine literature is enough to confirm this: that desperate night when a rural police sergeant, shouting that he would not condone the crime of killing a brave man, began to fight on the side of the deserter Martín Fierro against his own men.

For the European the world is a cosmos where each person corresponds intimately to the function he performs; for the Argentine it is a chaos. The European and the North American believe that a book which has been awarded any sort of prize must be good; the Argentine acknowledges the possibility that it may not be bad, in spite of the prize. In general, the Argentine is a skeptic. He may not know about the fable that says humanity always includes thirty-six just men—the Lamed Vovniks—who do not know each other but who secretly sustain the universe; if he hears that fable, he will not be surprised that those worthies are obscure and anonymous. His popular hero is the man who fights the multitude alone, either in action (Fierro, Moreira, Hormiga Negra), or in the mind or the past (Segundo Sombra). Other literatures do not record anything quite like that. For example, consider the case of two great European writers, Kipling and Franz Kafka. At first glance the two have nothing in common, but the principal theme of one is the vindication of order—of one order (the highway in *Kim*, the bridge in *The Bridge Builders*, the Roman wall in *Puck of Pook's Hill*); the principal theme of the other is the insupportable and tragic solitude of the person who lacks a place, even a most humble one, in the order of the universe.

Perhaps someone will say that the qualities I have mentioned are merely negative or anarchical ones, and will add that they are not capable of political application. I venture to suggest that the opposite is true. The most urgent problem of our time (already proclaimed with prophetical clarity by the almost forgotten Spencer) is the gradual interference of the State in the acts of the individual; in the struggle against this evil—called communism and fascism—Argentine individualism, which has perhaps been useless or even harmful up to now, would find justification and positive value.

Without hope and with nostalgia, I think of the abstract possibility of a political party that has some affinity with the Argentine character; a party that would promise us, say, a rigorous minimum of government.

Nationalism seeks to charm us, but the vision it presents is that of an infinitely importunate State; if that utopia were established on earth, it would have the providential virtue of making everyone desire, and finally achieve, its antithesis.

Buenos Aires, 1946

Quevedo

Like the history of the world, the history of literature abounds in enigmas. I found, and continue to find, none so disconcerting as the strange partial glory that has been accorded to Quevedo. His name does not appear on the lists of the world famous. I have made many attempts to discover why. Once, in a forgotten lecture, I thought I had found the reason: his crabbed pages did not encourage, even tolerate, the slightest expression of sentimentality. (George Moore has observed that sentimentality is the key to success.) On that occasion I said that a writer did not have to be sentimental to become famous, but that his work, or some aspect of his life, had to be marked by a certain pathetical quality. Neither Quevedo's life nor his art, I reflected, was distinguished by the sentimental excesses that usually spell success.

I do not know whether my explanation is correct. I should like to amplify it now, as follows: Quevedo, I believe, is inferior to no one, but he has not found a symbol that captures the popular imagination. Homer has Priam, who kisses the murderous hands of Achilles; Sophocles, a king who solves riddles and then is forced by the fates to resolve the horror of his own destiny; Lucretius, the infinite stellar abyss and the clashing of the atoms; Dante, the nine circles of hell and the Rose of Paradise; Shakespeare, his worlds of violence and music; Cervantes, the happy balance of Sancho and Quixote; Swift, his republic of virtuous horses and bestial Yahoos; Melville, the abomination and the love of the White Whale; Franz Kafka, his deepening and sordid labyrinths. No writer has attained universal fame without coining a symbol; but that symbol is not always objective and external. Góngora and Mallarmé are examples of the writer who laboriously creates a secret work; Whitman endures as the semi-divine protagonist of *Leaves of Grass*. But all that endures of Quevedo is a caricature. Leopoldo Lugones (*El imperio jesuítico*, 1904, p. 59) has observed that the most noble Spanish stylist has come to be identified as the prototype of the spicy anecdotist.

Lamb said that Edmund Spenser was the poet's poet. One would have to say that Quevedo is the writer's writer. To like Quevedo one must be (actually or potentially) a man of letters; conversely, no one with a literary vocation can fail to like Quevedo.

Quevedo's greatness is verbal. To consider him a philosopher, a theologian, or a statesman (as Aureliano Fernández Guerra attempts to do), is an error that may be justified by the titles but not the content of his works. His treatise entitled *Providencia de Dios, padecida de los que la niegan y gozada de los que la confiesan: doctrina estudiada en los gusanos y persecuciones de Job* is based on intimidation rather than reasoning. Like Cicero (*De natura deorum,* II, 40–44), he proves the existence of a divine order by the order observed in the stars, "the vast republic of lights," and after dismissing that stellar variation of the cosmological argument he adds: "Those who absolutely denied the existence of God were few; I shall expose to shame those who were shameless: Diagoras of Melos, sur-named the Atheist, Protagoras of Abdera, disciples of Democritus, and Bion of Borysthenes, a disciple of the obscene and deluded Theodorus," which is mere terrorism. In the history of philosophy are doctrines, probably false, that exercise an obscure charm on human imagination: the Platonic and Pythagorean doctrine of the transmigration of the soul through many bodies, the Gnostic doctrine that the world was created by a hostile or rudimentary god. Quevedo, merely a student of truth, is invulnerable to that charm. He writes that the transmigration of souls is "bestial foolishness" and "brutish folly." Empedocles of Agrigentum said: "I have been a boy, a girl, a plant, a bird, and a mute fish jumping out of the sea"; in *Provi-*

dencia de Dios Quevedo notes: "The self-styled judge and legislator of that conglomeration was Empedocles, a man so foolish that he said he had been a fish and then was transformed into such a contrary and different nature that he died as a butterfly on Mount Aetna; and in full view of the sea, his former home, he cast himself into the fire." Quevedo reviles the Gnostics as infamous, accursed, mad, and says they are inventors of nonsense (*Zahurdas de Plutón, in fine*).

Quevedo's *Política de Dios y gobierno de Cristo nuestro Señor* should be considered, Aureliano Fernández Guerra says, "as a complete system of government, the most perfect, noble, and appropriate one of all." To evaluate that opinion more effectively, let us remember that the forty-seven chapters of the book are based on the curious hypothesis that the actions and words of Christ (who was, it is known, *Rex Judaeorum*) are secret symbols that provide politicians with a key for solving their problems. Faithful to this cabala, Quevedo's interpretation of the parable of the Good Samaritan is that tributes demanded by kings must be small; he says that the parable of the loaves and fishes means kings must supply needs; and that the repetition of the formula *sequebantur* implies "the king must lead his ministers, not vice versa." Our surprise wavers between the arbitrariness of the method and the triviality of the conclusions. Quevedo, by the dignity of his expression, atones for everything, or almost.[1] Some readers may even find the work edifying. A similar dichotomy is observed in the *Marco Bruto*, where the thought is not memorable although the sentences are. The most imposing of Quevedo's styles attains perfection in that work. The Spanish of those lapidary pages seems to return to the arduous Latin of Seneca, Tacitus, and Lucan—the tortured and crabbed Latin of the *silver age*. The ostentatious laconism, the hyperbaton, the almost algebraic austerity, the juxtaposition of opposites, the dryness, the repetition of

[1] Reyes (*Capítulos de literatura española*, p. 133) correctly observes: "Quevedo's political works do not propose a new interpretation of political values, they are mainly interesting from a rhetorical standpoint today. . . . They are either occasional pamphlets, or works of academic declamation. Despite its ambitious format, the *Política de Dios* is nothing but a pronouncement against bad ministers. But some of Quevedo's most typical traits are to be found on its pages."

words, give this text an illusory precision. Many lines deserve, or demand, to be called perfect. This, for example:

A lineage was honored with laurel leaves; great and sovereign victories were acclaimed with shouts of triumph; lives that were almost divine were rewarded with a statue; and so that the wreaths and the shouting and the marble should not lose their connotation of glory, they were reserved only for merit, not pretension.

Quevedo frequented other styles with equal success: the apparently oral style of the *Buscón,* the outrageous and orgiastic (but not illogical) style of *La hora de todos.*

Chesterton has asserted that language is not a scientific achievement, but an artistic one; it was invented by warriors and hunters and is much earlier than science. Quevedo never believed that; for him language was, essentially, a logical instrument. The commonplaces or iterations of poetry—water compared to crystal, hands compared to snow, eyes that shine like stars, and stars that gaze down like eyes—annoyed him because they were facile, but much more because they were false. When he criticized them, he forgot that the metaphor is the momentary contact of two images, not the methodical likening of two things. . . . He also lashed out against certain ridiculous idioms. With the aim of "putting them to shame," he used the idioms to weave the rhapsody entitled *Cuento de cuentos.* Many generations, spellbound, have chosen to see in that *reductio ad absurdum* a veritable museum of beauty, divinely destined to save from oblivion such expressions as *zurriburri, abarrisco, cochite hervite, quitame allá esas pajas,* and *a trochi-moche.*

Quevedo has been compared to Lucian of Samosata on more than one occasion. One basic difference separates them: when Lucian attacked the Olympian divinities in the second century, he did so as a religious polemist; when Quevedo repeated that attack in the seventeenth century, he was merely observing a literary tradition.

Quevedo's poetry is as many-faceted as his prose. Considered as documents of passion, his erotic poems are unsatisfactory; but as exercises in hyperbole, as deliberate Petrarchan experiments, they are usually quite admirable. A man of vehement appetites, Quevedo continually aspired to attain a kind of stoic asceticism. He scoffed at those who became dependent on women ("wise is the man who uses his caresses for a purpose, and nothing more"). That explains the deliberate artificiality of Muse IV of his *Parnassus,* which "sings of exploits of love and beauty." Quevedo's personal accent is found in other poems, those that permit him to give vent to his melancholy, his anger, or his disenchantment. An example is this sonnet written in his Torre de Juan Abad, which he sent to Don José González de Salas (*Musa* II, 109):

> Retirado en la paz de estos desiertos,
> Con pocos, pero doctos, libros juntos,
> Vivo en conversación con los difuntos
> Y escucho con mis ojos a los muertos.

> Si no siempre entendidos, siempre abiertos,
> O enmiendan o secundan mis asuntos,
> Y en músicos callados contrapuntos
> Al sueño de la vida hablan despiertos.

> Las grandes almas que la muerte ausenta,
> De injurias de los años vengadora,
> Libra, oh gran don Joseph, docta la Imprenta.

> En fuga irrevocable huye la hora;
> Pero aquélla el mejor cálculo cuenta,
> Que en la lección y estudio nos mejora.

There are traces of *conceptismo* (the use of oxymoron) in this selection (listening with the eyes, posing wakeful questions to the dream-life), but the sonnet is effective in spite of them, not because of them. I shall not say that it is a transcription of reality, for reality is not verbal, but I can say that the words are less important than the scene they evoke or the virile accent that seems to inform them. But it is not always thus; in the most noteworthy sonnet of the volume— "Memoria immortal de don Pedro Girón, duque de Osuna, muerto en la prisión"—the splendid effect of the couplet

> Su Tumba son de Flandes las Campañas
> y su Epitaphio la sangrienta Luna

is felt before the interpretation and does not depend on it. I can say the same thing of the expression that follows: "the military weeping," the meaning of which is not enigmatic, but indeed trite: "the weeping of the military men." And as for "the bloody Moon," it is perhaps better not to know that it is the symbol of the Turks, eclipsed by certain of Don Pedro Téllez Girón's piracies.

Not infrequently Quevedo's point of departure is a classical text. For example, the memorable line (*Musa* IV, 31):

Polvo serán, mas polvo enamorado

is a re-creation, or exaltation, of a line by Propertius (*Elegies*, I, 19):

Ut meus oblito pulvis amore vacet.

The scope of Quevedo's poetical work is vast. It includes pensive sonnets, which reveal a prefiguring of Wordsworth; opaque and rasping severities;[2] brusque theological magic ("With the twelve I supped; I was the supper"); Gongorisms inserted to show that he could play that game too; pleasant Italianate urbanities ("solitude humble, sonorous, and green"); variations of Persius, Seneca, Juvenal, the Scriptures, and Joachim du Bellay; Latinate concisions; coarse jokes;[3] curious jests;[4] lugubrious commentaries on annihilation and chaos.

[2] Temblaron los umbrales y las puertas,
Donde la majestad negra y oscura
Las frías desangradas sombras muertas
Oprime en ley desesperada y dura;
Las tres gargantas al ladrido abiertas,
Viendo la nueva luz divina y pura,
Enmudeció Cerbero, y de repente
Hondos suspiros dió la negra gente.

Gimió debajo de los pies el suelo,
Desiertos montes de ceniza canos,
Que no merecen ver ojos del cielo,
Y en nuestra amarillez ciegan los llanos.
Acrecentaban miedo y desconsuelo
Los roncos perros, que en los reinos vanos
Molestan el silencio y los oídos,
Confundiendo lamentos y ladridos.
(*Musa* IX)

[3] La Méndez llegó chillando
Con trasudores de aceite,
Derramado por los hombros
El columpio de las liendres.
(*Musa* V)

[4] Aquesto Fabio cantaba
A los balcones y rejas
De Aminta, que aun de olvidarlo,
Le han dicho que no se acuerda.
(*Musa* VI)

41

Quevedo's best work transcends the motives that engendered it and the common ideas that inform it. It is not obscure. Unlike some writings by Mallarmé, Yeats, and George, it does not perturb or bewilder the reader with enigmas. Quevedo's works are (to find some way to express it) verbal objects, pure and independent like a sword or a silver ring. This one, for example:

> Harta la Toga del veneno tirio,
> O ya en el oro pálido y rigente
> Cubre con los thesoros del Oriente,
> Mas no descansa, ¡oh Licas!, tu martirio.
>
> Padeces un magnífico delirio,
> Cuando felicidad tan delincuente
> Tu horror oscuro en esplendor te miente,
> Víbora en rosicler, áspid en lirio.
>
> Competir su Palacio a Jove quieres,
> Pues miente el oro Estrellas a su modo,
> En el que vives, sin saber que mueres.
>
> Y en tantas glorias tú, señor de todo,
> Para quien sabe examinarte, eres
> Lo solamente vil, el asco, el lodo.

Three hundred years have passed since the corporal death of Quevedo, but he still continues to be the leading artisan of Hispanic letters. Like Joyce, like Goethe, like Shakespeare, like Dante—like no other writer—Francisco de Quevedo is less a man than a vast and complex literature.

Partial Enchantments of the *Quixote*

It is probable that these observations have been made before at least once and, perhaps, many times; the novelty of them interests me less than their possible truth.

In comparison with other classics (the *Iliad*, the *Aeneid*, the *Pharsalia*, the Dantesque *Comedy*, the tragedies and comedies of Shakespeare), the *Quixote* is realistic; but this realism differs essentially from the nineteenth-century variety. Joseph Conrad was able to write that he excluded the supernatural from his works, because to include it would seem to be a denial that the quotidian was marvelous. I do not know whether Miguel de Cervantes shared that idea, but I do know that the form of the *Quixote* caused him to counterpose a real, prosaic world with an imaginary, poetic one. Conrad and Henry James incorporated reality into their novels because they deemed it poetic; to Cervantes the real and the poetic are antonyms. To the vast and vague geography of the Amadís, he opposes the dusty roads and sordid inns of Castile; it is as if a novelist of our day were to sketch a satirical caricature of, say, service stations, treating them in a ludicrous way. Cervantes has created for us the poetry of seventeenth-century Spain, but neither that century nor that Spain were poetic for him; men like Unamuno or Azorín or Antonio Machado, whose emotions were stirred by the evocation of La Mancha, he would have found incomprehensible. The plan of his work precluded the marvelous, but still the marvelous had to be there, if only indirectly, as crime and mystery are present in a parody of the detective story. Cervantes could not have had recourse to amulets or sorcery, but he insinuated the supernatural in a subtle and therefore more effective way. In his heart of hearts, Cervantes loved the supernatural. In 1924 Paul Groussac observed: "With his cursory smattering of Latin and Italian, Cervantes derived his literary production primarily from pastoral novels and novels of chivalry, fables that had given solace to him in his captivity." The *Quixote* is less an antidote for those tales than a secret nostalgic farewell.

Every novel is an ideal depiction of reality. Cervantes delights in fusing the objective and the subjective, the world of the reader and the world of the book. In the chapters that consider whether the barber's basin is a helmet and the packsaddle a harness, the problem is treated explicitly; other parts, as I mentioned before, merely hint at it. In the sixth chapter of Part One the priest and the barber inspect Don Quixote's library; astonishingly enough, one of the books they examine is the *Galatea* by Cervantes. It develops that the barber is a friend of his who does not admire him very much, and says that Cervantes is more versed in misfortunes than in verses. He adds that the book has a rather well-constructed plot; it proposes something and concludes nothing. The barber, a dream of Cervantes or a form of one of Cervantes' dreams, passes judgment on Cervantes. It is also surprising to learn, at the beginning of Chapter IX, that the whole novel has been translated from the Arabic and that Cervantes acquired the manuscript in the marketplace of Toledo. It was translated by a Morisco, who lived in Cervantes' house for more than a month and a half while he completed the task. We are reminded of Carlyle, who feigned that the *Sartor Resartus* was a partial version of a work published in Germany by Dr. Diogenes Teufelsdröckh; we are reminded of the Spanish Rabbi Moisés de León, who wrote the *Zohar* or *Book of the Splendor* and divulged it as the work of a Palestinian rabbi of the third century.

The set of strange ambiguities culminates in Part Two. The pro-

44

tagonists of the *Quixote* who are, also, readers of the *Quixote,* have read Part One. Here we inevitably remember the case of Shakespeare, who includes on the stage of *Hamlet* another stage, where a tragedy almost like that of *Hamlet* is being presented. The imperfect correspondence of the principal work and the secondary one lessens the effectiveness of that inclusion. A device analogous to Cervantes' and even more startling, appears in the *Ramayana*, epic poem by Valmiki, which relates the deeds of Rama and his war with the evil spirits. In the last book Rama's children, not knowing who their father is, seek refuge in a forest, where a hermit teaches them to read. That teacher, strangely enough, is Valmiki; the book they study is the *Ramayana.* Rama orders a sacrifice of horses; Valmiki comes to the ceremony with his pupils. They sing the *Ramayana* to the accompaniment of the lute. Rama hears his own story, recognizes his children, and then rewards the poet.

Chance has caused something similar to occur in *A Thousand and One Nights.* That compilation of fantastic stories duplicates and reduplicates to the point of vertigo the ramification of a central tale into subordinate ones, without attempting to evaluate their realities; the effect (which should have been profound) is superficial, like that of a Persian rug. The first story is well known: the desolate oath of the Sultan, who marries a maiden each night and then orders her to be beheaded at dawn, and the courage of Scheherazade, who delights him with fables until a thousand and one nights have gyrated about them and she shows him their son. The need to complete a thousand and one sections obliged the copyists of the work to make all sorts of interpolations. None is so disturbing as that of night DCII, magic among the nights. That is when the Sultan hears his own story from the Sultana's mouth. He hears the beginning of the story, which embraces all the other stories as well as—monstrously—itself. Does the reader perceive the unlimited possibilities of that interpolation, the curious danger—that the Sultana may persist and the Sultan, transfixed, will hear forever the truncated story of *A Thousand and One Nights,* now infinite and circular?

The inventions of philosophy are no less fantastic than those of art. In the first volume of *The World and the Individual* (1899) Josiah Royce has formulated the following one:

. . . let us suppose, if you please, that a portion of the surface of England is very perfectly levelled and smoothed, and is then devoted to the production of our precise map of England. . . . But now suppose that this our resemblance is to be made absolutely exact, in the sense previously defined. A map of England, contained within England, is to represent, down to the minutest detail, every contour and marking, natural or artificial, that occurs upon the surface of England . . . For the map, in order to be complete, according to the rule given, will have to contain, as a part of itself, a representation of its own contour and contents. In order that this representation should be constructed, the representation itself will have to contain once more, as a part of itself, a representation of its own contour and contents; and this representation, in order to be exact, will have once more to contain an image of itself; and so on without limit.

Why does it make us uneasy to know that the map is within the map and the thousand and one nights are within the book of *A Thousand and One Nights*? Why does it disquiet us to know that Don Quixote is a reader of the *Quixote*, and Hamlet is a spectator of *Hamlet*? I believe I have found the answer: those inversions suggest that if the characters in a story can be readers or spectators, then we, their readers or spectators, can be fictitious. In 1833 Carlyle observed that universal history is an infinite sacred book that all men write and read and try to understand, and in which they too are written.

Nathaniel Hawthorne[1]

I shall begin the history of American literature with the history of a metaphor; or rather, with some examples of that metaphor. I don't know who invented it; perhaps it is a mistake to suppose that metaphors can be invented. The real ones, those that formulate intimate connections between one image and another, have always existed; those we can still invent are the false ones, which are not worth inventing. The metaphor I am speaking of is the one that compares dreams to a theatrical performance. Quevedo used it in the seventeenth century at the beginning of the *Sueño de la muerte*; Luis de Góngora made it a part of the sonnet "Varia imaginación," where we read:

> A dream is a playwright
> Clothed in beautiful shadows
> In a theatre fashioned on the wind.

In the eighteenth century Addison will say it more precisely. When the soul dreams (he writes) it is the theatre, the actors, and the audience. Long before, the Persian Omar Khayyām had written that the history of the world is a play that God—the multiform God of the

[1] This is the text of a lecture given at the Colegio Libre de Estudios Superiores in March, 1949.

pantheists—contrives, enacts, and beholds to entertain his eternity; long afterward, Jung the Swiss in charming and doubtless accurate volumes compares literary inventions to oneiric inventions, literature to dreams.

If literature is a dream (a controlled and deliberate dream, but fundamentally a dream) then Góngora's verses would be an appropriate epigraph to this story about American literature, and a look at Hawthorne, the dreamer, would be a good beginning. There are other American writers before him—Fenimore Cooper, a sort of Eduardo Gutiérrez infinitely inferior to Eduardo Gutiérrez; Washington Irving, a contriver of pleasant Spanish fantasies—but we can skip over them without any consequence.

Hawthorne was born in 1804 in the port of Salem, which suffered, even then, from two traits that were anomalous in America: it was a very old, but poor, city; it was a city in decadence. Hawthorne lived in that old and decaying city with the honest biblical name until 1836; he loved it with the sad love inspired by persons who do not love us, or by failures, illness, and manias; essentially it is not untrue to say that he never left his birthplace. Fifty years later, in London or Rome, he continued to live in his Puritan town of Salem; for example, when he denounced sculptors (remember that this was in the nineteenth century) for making nude statues.

His father, Captain Nathaniel Hawthorne, died in Surinam in 1808 of yellow fever; one of his ancestors, John Hawthorne, had been a judge in the witchcraft trials of 1692, in which nineteen women, among them the slave girl Tituba, were condemned to be executed by hanging. In those curious trials (fanaticism has assumed other forms in our time) Justice Hawthorne acted with severity and probably with sincerity. Nathaniel, our Nathaniel, wrote that his ancestor made himself so conspicuous in the martyrdom of the witches that possibly the blood of those unfortunate women had left a stain on him, a stain so deep as to be present still on his old bones in the Charter Street Cemetery if they had not yet turned to dust. After that picturesque note Hawthorne added that, not knowing whether his elders had repented and begged for divine mercy, he wished to do so in their name, begging that any curse that had fallen on their descendants would be pardoned from that day forward.

48

When Captain Hawthorne died, his widow, Nathaniel's mother, became a recluse in her bedroom on the second floor. The rooms of his sisters, Louise and Elizabeth, were on the same floor; Nathaniel's was on the top floor. The family did not eat together and they scarcely spoke to one another; their meals were left on trays in the hall. Nathaniel spent his days writing fantastic stories; at dusk he would go out for a walk. His furtive way of life lasted for twelve years. In 1837 he wrote to Longfellow: ". . . I have secluded myself from society; and yet I never meant any such thing, nor dreamed what sort of life I was going to lead. I have made a captive of myself, and put me into a dungeon, and now I cannot find the key to let myself out."

Hawthorne was tall, handsome, lean, dark. He walked with the rocking gait of a seaman. At that time children's literature did not exist (fortunately for boys and girls!). Hawthorne had read *Pilgrim's Progress* at the age of six; the first book he bought with his own money was *The Faërie Queene*; two allegories. Also, although his biographers may not say so, he read the Bible; perhaps the same Bible that the first Hawthorne, William Hathorne, brought from England with a sword in 1630. I have used the word "allegories"; the word is important, perhaps imprudent or indiscreet, to use when speaking of the work of Hawthorne. It is common knowledge that Edgar Allan Poe accused Hawthorne of allegorizing and that Poe deemed both the activity and the genre indefensible. Two tasks confront us: first, to ascertain whether the allegorical genre is, in fact, illicit; second, to ascertain whether Nathaniel Hawthorne's works belong to that category.

The best refutation of allegories I know is Croce's; the best vindication, Chesterton's. Croce says that the allegory is a tiresome pleonasm, a collection of useless repetitions which shows us (for example) Dante led by Virgil and Beatrice and then explains to us, or gives us to understand, that Dante is the soul, Virgil is philosophy or reason or natural intelligence, and Beatrice is theology or grace. According to Croce's argument (the example is not his), Dante's first step was to think: "Reason and faith bring about the salvation of souls" or "Philosophy and theology lead us to heaven" and then, for *reason* or *philosophy* he substituted *Virgil* and for *faith* or *theology* he put *Beatrice,* all of which became a kind of masquerade. By

49

that derogatory definition an allegory would be a puzzle, more extensive, boring, and unpleasant than other puzzles. It would be a barbaric or puerile genre, an aesthetic sport. Croce wrote that refutation in 1907; Chesterton had already refuted him in 1904 without Croce's knowing it. How vast and uncommunicative is the world of literature!

The page from Chesterton to which I refer is part of a monograph on the artist Watts, who was famous in England at the end of the nineteenth century and was accused, like Hawthorne, of allegorism. Chesterton admits that Watts has produced allegories, but he denies that the genre is censurable. He reasons that reality is interminably rich and that the language of men does not exhaust that vertiginous treasure. He writes:

Man knows that there are in the soul tints more bewildering, more numberless, and more nameless than the colours of an autumn forest; . . . Yet he seriously believes that these things can every one of them, in all their tones and semi-tones, in all their blends and unions, be accurately represented by an arbitrary system of grunts and squeals. He believes that an ordinary civilized stockbroker can really produce out of his own inside noises which denote all the mysteries of memory and all the agonies of desire.

Later Chesterton infers that various languages can somehow correspond to the ungraspable reality, and among them are allegories and fables.

In other words, Beatrice is not an emblem of faith, a belabored and arbitrary synonym of the word *faith*. The truth is that something—a peculiar sentiment, an intimate process, a series of analogous states —exists in the world that can be indicated by two symbols: one, quite insignificant, the sound of the word *faith*; the other, Beatrice, the glorious Beatrice who descended from Heaven and left her footprints in Hell to save Dante. I don't know whether Chesterton's thesis is valid; I do know that the less an allegory can be reduced to a plan, to a cold set of abstractions, the better it is. One writer thinks in images (Shakespeare or Donne or Victor Hugo, say), and another writer thinks in abstractions (Benda or Bertrand Russell); a priori, the former are just as estimable as the latter. However, when an

50

abstract man, a reasoner, also wants to be imaginative, or to pass as such, then the allegory denounced by Croce occurs. We observe that a logical process has been embellished and disguised by the author to dishonor the reader's understanding, as Wordsworth said. A famous example of that ailment is the case of José Ortega y Gasset, whose good thought is obstructed by difficult and adventitious metaphors; many times this is true of Hawthorne. Outside of that, the two writers are antagonistic. Ortega can reason, well or badly, but he cannot imagine; Hawthorne was a man of continual and curious imagination; but he was refractory, so to speak, to reason. I am not saying he was stupid; I say that he thought in images, in intuitions, as women usually think, not with a dialectical mechanism.

One aesthetic error debased him: the Puritan desire to make a fable out of each imagining induced him to add morals and sometimes to falsify and to deform them. The notebooks in which he jotted down ideas for plots have been preserved; in one of them, dated 1836, he wrote: "A snake taken into a man's stomach and nourished there from fifteen years to thirty-five, tormenting him most horribly." That is enough, but Hawthorne considers himself obliged to add: "A type of envy or some other evil passion." Another example, this time from 1838: "A series of strange, mysterious, dreadful events to occur, wholly destructive of a person's happiness. He to impute them to various persons and causes, but ultimately finds that he is himself the sole agent. Moral, that our welfare depends on ourselves." Another, from the same year: "A person, while awake and in the business of life, to think highly of another, and place perfect confidence in him, but to be troubled with dreams in which this seeming friend appears to act the part of a most deadly enemy. Finally it is discovered that the dream-character is the true one. The explanation would be—the soul's instinctive perception." Better are those pure fantasies that do not look for a justification or moral and that seem to have no other substance than an obscure terror. Again, from 1838: "The situation of a man in the midst of a crowd, yet as completely in the power of another, life and all, as if they two were in the deepest solitude." The following, which Hawthorne noted five years later, is a variation of the above: "Some man of powerful character to command a person, morally subjected to him, to perform some act. The

51

commanding person to suddenly die; and, for all the rest of his life, the subjected one continues to perform that act." (I don't know how Hawthorne would have written that story. I don't know if he would have decided that the act performed should be trivial or slightly horrible or fantastic or perhaps humiliating.) This one also has slavery—subjection to another—as its theme: "A rich man left by will his mansion and estate to a poor couple. They remove into it, and find there a darksome servant, whom they are forbidden by will to turn away. He becomes a torment to them; and, in the finale, he turns out to be the former master of the estate." I shall mention two more sketches, rather curious ones; their theme, not unknown to Pirandello or André Gide, is the coincidence or the confusion of the aesthetic plane and the common plane, of art and reality. The first one: "Two persons to be expecting some occurrence, and watching for the two principal actors in it, and to find that the occurrence is even then passing, and that they themselves are the two actors." The other is more complex: "A person to be writing a tale, and to find that it shapes itself against his intentions; that the characters act otherwise than he thought; that unforeseen events occur; and a catastrophe comes which he strives in vain to avert. It might shadow forth his own fate—he having made himself one of the personages." These games, these momentary confluences of the imaginative world and the real world—the world we pretend is real when we read—are, or seem to us, modern. Their origin, their ancient origin, is perhaps to be found in that part of the *Iliad* in which Helen of Troy weaves into her tapestry the battles and the disasters of the Trojan War even then in progress. Virgil must have been impressed by that passage, for the *Aeneid* relates that Aeneas, hero of the Trojan War, arrived at the port of Carthage and saw scenes from the war sculptured on the marble of a temple and, among the many images of warriors, he saw his own likeness. Hawthorne liked those contacts of the imaginary and the real, those reflections and duplications of art; and in the sketches I have mentioned we observe that he leaned toward the pantheistic notion that one man is the others, that one man is all men.

Something more serious than duplications and pantheism is seen in the sketches, something more serious for a man who aspires to be a novelist, I mean. It is that, in general, situations were Hawthorne's stimulus, Hawthorne's point of departure—situations, not characters. Hawthorne first imagined, perhaps unwittingly, a situation and then sought the characters to embody it. I am not a novelist, but I suspect that few novelists have proceeded in that fashion. "I believe that Schomberg is real," wrote Joseph Conrad about one of the most memorable characters in his novel *Victory,* and almost any novelist could honestly say that about any of his characters. The adventures of the *Quixote* are not so well planned, the slow and antithetical dialogues—reasonings, I believe the author calls them—offend us by their improbability, but there is no doubt that Cervantes knew Don Quixote well and could believe in him. Our belief in the novelist's belief makes up for any negligence or defect in the work. What does it matter if the episodes are unbelievable or awkward when we realize that the author planned them, not to challenge our credibility, but to define his characters? What do we care about the puerile scandals and the confused crimes of the hypothetical Court of Denmark if we believe in Prince Hamlet? But Hawthorne first conceived a situation, or a series of situations, and then elaborated the people his plan required. That method can produce, or tolerate, admirable stories because their brevity makes the plot more visible than the actors, but not admirable novels, where the general form (if there is one) is visible only at the end and a single badly invented character can contaminate the others with unreality. From the foregoing statement it will be inferred that Hawthorne's stories are better than Hawthorne's novels. I believe that is true. The twenty-four chapters of *The Scarlet Letter* abound in memorable passages, written in good and sensitive prose, but none of them has moved me like the singular story of "Wakefield" in the *Twice-Told Tales.*

Hawthorne had read in a newspaper, or pretended for literary reasons that he had read in a newspaper, the case of an Englishman who left his wife without cause, took lodgings in the next street and there, without anyone's suspecting it, remained hidden for twenty years. During that long period he spent all his days across from his house or watched it from the corner, and many times he caught a glimpse of his wife. When they had given him up for dead, when his wife had been resigned to widowhood for a long time, the man opened the door of his house one day and walked in—simply, as if he had

53

been away only a few hours. (To the day of his death he was an exemplary husband.) Hawthorne read about the curious case uneasily and tried to understand it, to imagine it. He pondered on the subject; "Wakefield" is the conjectural story of that exile. The interpretations of the riddle can be infinite; let us look at Hawthorne's.

He imagines Wakefield to be a calm man, timidly vain, selfish, given to childish mysteries and the keeping of insignificant secrets; a dispassionate man of great imaginative and mental poverty, but capable of long, leisurely, inconclusive, and vague meditations; a constant husband, by virtue of his laziness. One October evening Wakefield bids farewell to his wife. He tells her—we must not forget we are at the beginning of the nineteenth century—that he is going to take the stagecoach and will return, at the latest, within a few days. His wife, who knows he is addicted to inoffensive mysteries, does not ask the reason for the trip. Wakefield is wearing boots, a rain hat, and an overcoat; he carries an umbrella and a valise. Wakefield—and this surprises me—does not yet know what will happen. He goes out, more or less firm in his decision to disturb or to surprise his wife by being away from home for a whole week. He goes out, closes the front door, then half opens it, and, for a moment, smiles. Years later his wife will remember that last smile. She will imagine him in a coffin with the smile frozen on his face, or in paradise, in glory, smiling with cunning and tranquility. Everyone will believe he has died but she will remember that smile and think that perhaps she is not a widow.

Going by a roundabout way, Wakefield reaches the lodging place where he has made arrangements to stay. He makes himself comfortable by the fireplace and smiles; he is one street away from his house and has arrived at the end of his journey. He doubts; he congratulates himself; he finds it incredible to be there already; he fears that he may have been observed and that someone may inform on him. Almost repentant, he goes to bed, stretches out his arms in the vast emptiness and says aloud: "I will not sleep alone another night." The next morning he awakens earlier than usual and asks himself, in amazement, what he is going to do. He knows that he has some purpose, but he has difficulty defining it. Finally he realizes that his

54

purpose is to discover the effect that one week of widowhood will have on the virtuous Mrs. Wakefield. His curiosity forces him into the street. He murmurs, "I shall spy on my home from a distance." He walks, unaware of his direction; suddenly he realizes that force of habit has brought him, like a traitor, to his own door and that he is about to enter it. Terrified, he turns away. Have they seen him? Will they pursue him? At the corner he turns back and looks at his house; it seems different to him now, because he is already another man—a single night has caused a transformation in him, although he does not know it. The moral change that will condemn him to twenty years of exile has occurred in his soul. Here, then, is the beginning of the long adventure. Wakefield acquires a reddish wig. He changes his habits; soon he has established a new routine. He is troubled by the suspicion that his absence has not disturbed Mrs. Wakefield enough. He decides he will not return until he has given her a good scare. One day the druggist enters the house, another day the doctor. Wakefield is sad, but he fears that his sudden reappearance may aggravate the illness. Obsessed, he lets time pass; before he had thought, "I shall return in a few days," but now he thinks, "in a few weeks." And so ten years pass. For a long time he has not known that his conduct is strange. With all the lukewarm affection of which his heart is capable, Wakefield continues to love his wife, while she is forgetting him. One Sunday morning the two meet in the street amid the crowds of London. Wakefield has become thin; he walks obliquely, as though hiding or escaping; his low forehead is deeply wrinkled; his face, which was common before, is extraordinary, because of his extraordinary conduct. His small eyes wander or look inward. His wife has grown stout; she is carrying a prayer book and her whole person seems to symbolize a placid and resigned widowhood. She is accustomed to sadness and would not exchange it, perhaps, for joy. Face to face, the two look into each other's eyes. The crowd separates them, and soon they are lost within it. Wakefield hurries to his lodgings, bolts the door, and throws himself on the bed where he is seized by a fit of sobbing. For an instant he sees the miserable oddity of his life. "Wakefield, Wakefield! You are mad!" he says to himself.

Perhaps he is. In the center of London he has severed his ties with the world. Without having died, he has renounced his place and his privileges among living men. Mentally he continues to live with his wife in his home. He does not know, or almost never knows, that he is a different person. He keeps saying, "I shall soon go back," and he does not realize that he has been repeating these words for twenty years. In his memory the twenty years of solitude seem to be an interlude, a mere parenthesis. One afternoon, an afternoon like other afternoons, like the thousands of previous afternoons, Wakefield looks at his house. He sees that they have lighted the fire in the second-floor bedroom; grotesquely, the flames project Mrs. Wakefield's shadow on the ceiling. Rain begins to fall, and Wakefield feels a gust of cold air. Why should he get wet when his house, his home, is there. He walks heavily up the steps and opens the door. The crafty smile we already know is hovering, ghostlike, on his face. At last Wakefield has returned. Hawthorne does not tell us of his subsequent fate, but lets us guess that he was already dead, in a sense. I quote the final words: "Amid the seeming confusion of our mysterious world, individuals are so nicely adjusted to a system, and systems to one another, and to a whole, that by stepping aside for a moment a man exposes himself to a fearful risk of losing his place for ever. Like Wakefield, he may become, as it were, the Outcast of the Universe."

In that brief and ominous parable, which dates from 1835, we have already entered the world of Herman Melville, of Kafka—a world of enigmatic punishments and indecipherable sins. You may say that there is nothing strange about that, since Kafka's world is Judaism, and Hawthorne's, the wrath and punishments of the Old Testament. That is a just observation, but it applies only to ethics, and the horrible story of Wakefield and many stories by Kafka are united not only by a common ethic but also by a common rhetoric. For example, the protagonist's profound *triviality*, which contrasts with the magnitude of his perdition and delivers him, even more helpless, to the Furies. There is the murky background against which the nightmare is etched. Hawthorne invokes a romantic past in other stories, but the scene of this tale is middle-class London, whose crowds serve, moreover, to conceal the hero.

Here, without any discredit to Hawthorne, I should like to insert an observation. The circumstance, the strange circumstance, of perceiving in a story written by Hawthorne at the beginning of the nineteenth century the same quality that distinguishes the stories Kafka wrote at the beginning of the twentieth must not cause us to forget that Hawthorne's particular quality has been created, or determined, by Kafka. "Wakefield" prefigures Franz Kafka, but Kafka modifies and refines the reading of "Wakefield." The debt is mutual; a great writer creates his precursors. He creates and somehow justifies them. What, for example, would Marlowe be without Shakespeare?

The translator and critic Malcolm Cowley sees in "Wakefield" an allegory of Nathaniel Hawthorne's curious life of reclusion. Schopenhauer has written the famous words to the effect that no act, no thought, no illness is involuntary; if there is any truth in that opinion, it would be valid to conjecture that Nathaniel Hawthorne left the society of other human beings for many years so that the singular story of Wakefield would exist in the universe, whose purpose may be variety. If Kafka had written that story, Wakefield would never have returned to his home; Hawthorne lets him return, but his return is no less lamentable or less atrocious than is his long absence.

One of Hawthorne's parables which was almost masterly, but not quite, because a preoccupation with ethics mars it, is "Earth's Holocaust." In that allegorical story Hawthorne foresees a moment when men, satiated by useless accumulations, resolve to destroy the past. They congregate at evening on one of the vast western plains of America to accomplish the feat. Men come from all over the world. They make a gigantic bonfire kindled with all the genealogies, all the diplomas, all the medals, all the orders, all the judgments, all the coats of arms, all the crowns, all the sceptres, all the tiaras, all the purple robes of royalty, all the canopies, all the thrones, all the spirituous liquors, all the bags of coffee, all the boxes of tea, all the cigars, all the love letters, all the artillery, all the swords, all the flags, all the martial drums, all the instruments of torture, all the guillotines, all the gallows trees, all the precious metals, all the money, all the titles of property, all the constitutions and codes of law, all the books, all the miters, all the vestments, all the sacred writings that populate and fatigue the Earth. Hawthorne views the conflagration with astonishment and even shock. A man of serious mien tells him that he should be neither glad nor sad, because the vast pyramid of fire has consumed only what was consumable. Another spectator—the Devil—

57

observes that the organizers of the holocaust have forgotten to throw away the essential element—the human heart—where the root of all sin resides, and that they have destroyed only a few forms. Hawthorne concludes as follows:

The heart, the heart—there was the little yet boundless sphere wherein existed the original wrong of which the crime and misery of this outward world were merely types. Purify that inward sphere, and the many shapes of evil that haunt the outward, and which now seem almost our only realities, will turn to shadowy phantoms and vanish of their own accord; but if we go no deeper than the intellect, and strive, with merely that feeble instrument, to discern and rectify what is wrong, our whole accomplishment will be a dream, so unsubstantial that it matters little whether the bonfire, which I have so faithfully described, were what we choose to call a real event and a flame that would scorch the finger, or only a phosphoric radiance and a parable of my own brain.

Here Hawthorne has allowed himself to be influenced by the Christian, and specifically the Calvinist, doctrine of the inborn depravation of mankind and does not appear to have noticed that his parable of an illusory destruction of all things can have a philosophical as well as a moral interpretation. For if the world is the dream of Someone, if there is Someone who is dreaming us now and who dreams the history of the universe (that is the doctrine of the idealists), then the annihilation of religions and the arts, the general burning of libraries, does not matter much more than does the destruction of the trappings of a dream. The Mind that dreamed them once will dream them again; as long as the Mind continues to dream, nothing will be lost. The belief in this truth, which seems fantastic, caused Schopenhauer, in his book *Parerga und Paralipomena*, to compare history to a kaleidoscope, in which the figures, not the pieces of glass, change; and to an eternal and confused tragicomedy in which the roles and masks, but not the actors, change. The presentiment that the universe is a projection of our soul and that universal history lies within each man induced Emerson to write the poem entitled "History."

As for the fantasy of abolishing the past, perhaps it is worth remembering that this was attempted in China, with adverse fortune, three centuries before Christ. Herbert Allen Giles wrote that the prime minister Li Su proposed that history should begin with the new monarch, who took the title of First Emperor. To sever the vain pretensions of antiquity, all books (except those that taught agriculture, medicine, or astrology) were decreed confiscated and burned. Persons who concealed their books were branded with a hot iron and forced to work on the construction of the Great Wall. Many valuable works were destroyed; posterity owes the preservation of the Confucius canon to the abnegation and valor of obscure and unknown men of letters. It is said that so many intellectuals were executed for defying the imperial edict that melons grew in winter on the burial ground.

Around the middle of the seventeenth century that same plan appeared in England, this time among the Puritans, Hawthorne's ancestors. Samuel Johnson relates that in one of the popular parliaments convoked by Cromwell it was seriously proposed that the archives of the Tower of London be burned, that every memory of the past be erased, and that a whole new way of life should be started. In other words, the plan to abolish the past had already occurred to men and —paradoxically—is therefore one of the proofs that the past cannot be abolished. The past is indestructible; sooner or later all things will return, including the plan to abolish the past.

Like Stevenson, also the son of Puritans, Hawthorne never ceased to feel that the task of the writer was frivolous or, what is worse, even sinful. In the preface to *The Scarlet Letter* he imagines that the shadows of his forefathers are watching him write his novel. It is a curious passage. "What is he?" says one ancient shadow to the other. "A writer of story-books! What kind of a business in life—what mode of glorifying God, or being serviceable to mankind in his day and generation—may that be? Why, the degenerate fellow might as well have been a fiddler!" The passage is curious, because it is in the nature of a confidence and reveals intimate scruples. It harks back to the ancient dispute between ethics and aesthetics or, if you prefer, theology and aesthetics. One early example of this dispute was in the Holy Scriptures and forbade men to adore idols. Another example, by Plato, was in the *Republic*, Book X: "God creates the Archetype (the original idea) of the table; the carpenter makes an imitation of the Archetype; the painter, an imitation of the imitation." Another is by Mohammed, who declared that every representation of a living thing will appear before the Lord on the day of the Last Judgment. The angels will order the artisan to animate what he has made; he will fail to do so and they will cast him into Hell for a certain length of time. Some Moslem teachers maintain that only images that can project a shadow (sculptured images) are forbidden. Plotinus was said to be ashamed to dwell in a body, and he did not permit sculptors to perpetuate his features. Once, when a friend urged him to have his portrait painted, he replied, "It is enough to be obliged to drag around this image in which nature has imprisoned me. But why shall I consent to the perpetuation of the image of this image?"

Nathaniel Hawthorne solved that difficulty (which is not a mere illusion). His solution was to compose moralities and fables; he made or tried to make art a function of the conscience. So, to use only one example, the novel *The House of the Seven Gables* attempts to show that the evil committed by one generation endures and persists in its descendants, like a sort of inherited punishment. Andrew Lang has compared it to Émile Zola's novels, or to Émile Zola's theory of novels; to me the only advantage to be gained by the juxtaposition of those heterogeneous names is the momentary surprise it causes us to experience. The fact that Hawthorne pursued, or tolerated, a moral purpose does not invalidate, cannot invalidate his work. In the course of a lifetime dedicated less to living than to reading, I have been able to verify repeatedly that aims and literary theories are nothing but stimuli; the finished work frequently ignores and even contradicts them. If the writer has something of value within him, no aim, however trite or erroneous it may be, will succeed in affecting his work irreparably. An author may suffer from absurd prejudices, but it will be impossible for his work to be absurd if it is genuine, if it responds to a genuine vision. Around 1916 the novelists of England and France believed (or thought they believed) that all Germans were devils; but they presented them as human beings in their novels. In Hawthorne the germinal vision was always true; what is false, what is ultimately false, are the moralities he added in the last paragraph or the characters he conceived, or assembled, in order to represent that vision. The characters in *The Scarlet Letter*—especially Hester Prynne, the heroine—are more independent, more autonomous, than those in his other stories; they are more like the inhabitants of most novels and not mere projections of Hawthorne, thinly disguised. This objectivity, this relative and partial objectivity, is perhaps the reason why two such acute (and dissimilar) writers as Henry James and Ludwig Lewisohn called *The Scarlet Letter* Hawthorne's masterpiece, his definitive testimony. But I would venture to differ with those two authorities. If a person longs for objectivity, if he hungers and thirsts for objectivity, let him look for it in Joseph Conrad or Tolstoi; if a person looks for the peculiar flavor of Nathaniel Hawthorne, he will be less apt to find it in the laborious novels than on some random page or in the trifling and pathetic stories. I don't know exactly how to justify my difference of opinion; in the three American novels and *The Marble Faun* I see only a series of situations, planned with professional skill to affect the reader, not a spontaneous and lively activity of the imagination. The imagination (I repeat) has planned the general plot and the digressions, not the weaving together of the episodes and the psychology—we have to call it by some name —of the actors.

Johnson observes that no writer likes to owe something to his contemporaries; Hawthorne was as unaware of them as possible. Perhaps he did the right thing; perhaps our contemporaries—always—seem too much like us, and if we are looking for new things we shall find them more easily in the ancients. According to his biographers, Hawthorne did not read De Quincey, did not read Keats, did not read Victor Hugo—who did not read each other, either. Groussac would not admit that an American could be original; he denounced "the notable influence of Hoffmann" on Hawthorne, an opinion that appears to be based on an impartial ignorance of both writers. Hawthorne's imagination is romantic; in spite of certain excesses, his style belongs to the eighteenth century, to the feeble end of the admirable eighteenth century.

I have quoted several fragments from the journal Hawthorne kept to entertain his long hours of solitude; I have given brief résumés of two stories; now I shall quote a page from *The Marble Faun* so that you may read Hawthorne's own words. The subject is that abyss or well that opened up, according to Latin historians, in the center of the Forum; a Roman, armed and on horseback, threw himself into its blind depths to propitiate the gods. Hawthorne's text reads as follows:

"Let us settle it," said Kenyon, "that this is precisely the spot where the chasm opened, into which Curtius precipitated his good steed and himself. Imagine the great, dusky gap, impenetrably deep, and with half-shaped monsters and hideous faces looming upward out of it, to the vast affright of the good citizens who peeped over the brim! Within it, beyond a question, there were prophetic visions,—intimations of all the future calamities of Rome,—shades of Goths, and Gauls, and even of the French soldiers of today. It was a pity to close it up so soon! I would give much for a peep into such a chasm."

"I fancy," remarked Miriam, "that every person takes a peep into it in moments of gloom and despondency; that is to say, in his moments of deepest insight.

"The chasm was merely one of the orifices of that pit of blackness that lies beneath us, everywhere. The firmest substance of human happiness is but a thin crust spread over it, with just reality enough to bear up the illusive stage-scenery amid which we tread. It needs no earthquake to open the chasm. A footstep, a little heavier than ordinary, will serve; and we must step very daintily, not to break through the crust at any moment. By and by, we inevitably sink! It was a foolish piece of heroism in Curtius to precipitate himself there, in advance; for all Rome, you see, has been swallowed up in that gulf, in spite of him. The Palace of the Caesars has gone down thither, with a hollow, rumbling sound of its fragments! All the temples have tumbled into it; and thousands of statues have been thrown after! All the armies and the triumphs have marched into the great chasm, with their martial music playing, as they stepped over the brink . . ."

From the standpoint of reason, of mere reason—which should not interfere with art—the fervent passage I have quoted is indefensible. The fissure that opened in the middle of the Forum is too many things. In the course of a single paragraph it is the crevice mentioned by Latin historians and it is also the mouth of Hell "with half-shaped monsters and hideous faces"; it is the essential horror of human life; it is Time, which devours statues and armies, and Eternity, which embraces all time. It is a multiple symbol, a symbol that is capable of many, perhaps incompatible, values. Such values can be offensive to reason, to logical understanding, but not to dreams, which have their singular and secret algebra, and in whose ambiguous realm one thing may be many. Hawthorne's world is the world of dreams. Once he planned to write a dream, "which shall resemble the real course of a dream, with all its inconsistency, its eccentricities and aimlessness," and he was amazed that no one had ever done such a thing before. The same journal in which he wrote about that strange plan—which our "modern" literature tries vainly to achieve and which, perhaps, has only been achieved by Lewis Carroll—contains his notes on thousands of trivial impressions, small concrete details (the movement of a hen, the shadow of a branch on the wall); they fill six volumes and their inexplicable abundance is the consternation of all his biographers. "They read like a series of very pleasant, though rather dullish and decidedly formal, letters, addressed to himself by a man who, having suspicions that they might be opened in the post, should have determined to insert nothing compromising." Henry James wrote that, with obvious perplexity. I believe that Nathaniel Hawthorne recorded those trivialities over the years to show himself that he was real, to free himself, somehow, from the impression of unreality, of ghostliness, that usually visited him.

One day in 1840 he wrote:

Here I sit in my old accustomed chamber, where I used to sit in days gone by . . . Here I have written many tales—many that have been burned to ashes, many that have doubtless deserved the same fate. This claims to be called a haunted chamber, for thousands upon thousands of visions have appeared to me in it; and some few of them have become visible to the world . . . And sometimes it seems to me as if I were already in the grave, with only life enough to be chilled and benumbed. But oftener I was happy . . . And now I begin to understand why I was imprisoned so many years in this lonely chamber, and why I could never break through the viewless bolts and bars; for if I had sooner made my escape into the world, I should have grown hard and rough, and been covered with earthly dust, and my heart might have become callous . . . Indeed, we are but shadows . . ."

In the lines I have just quoted, Hawthorne mentions "thousands upon thousands of visions." Perhaps this is not an exaggeration; the twelve volumes of Hawthorne's complete works include more than a hundred stories, and those are only a few of the very many he outlined in his journal. (Among the stories he finished, one—"Mr. Higginbotham's Catastrophe"—prefigures the detective story that Poe was to invent.)

Miss Margaret Fuller, who knew him in the utopian community of Brook Farm, wrote later, "Of that ocean we have had only a few drops," and Emerson, who was also a friend of his, thought Hawthorne had never given his full measure. Hawthorne married in 1842, when he was thirty-eight; until that time his life had been almost purely imaginative, mental. He worked in the Boston customhouse; he served as United States consul at Liverpool; he lived in Florence, Rome, and London. But his reality was always the filmy twilight, or lunar world, of the fantastic imagination.

At the beginning of this essay I mentioned the doctrine of the psychologist Jung, who compared literary inventions to oneiric inventions, or literature to dreams. That doctrine does not seem to be applicable to the literatures written in the Spanish language, which deal in dictionaries and rhetoric, not fantasy. On the other hand, it does pertain to the literature of North America, which (like the literatures of England or Germany) tends more toward invention than transcription, more toward creation than observation. Perhaps that is the reason for the curious veneration North Americans render to realistic works, which induces them to postulate, for example, that Maupassant is more important than Hugo. It is within the power of a North American writer to be Hugo, but not, without violence, Maupassant. In comparison with the literature of the United States, which has produced several men of genius and has had its influence felt in England and France, our Argentine literature may possibly seem somewhat provincial. Nevertheless, in the nineteenth century we produced some admirable works of realism—by Echeverría, Ascasubi, Hernández, and the forgotten Eduardo Gutiérrez—the North Americans have not surpassed (perhaps have not equaled) them to this day. Someone will object that Faulkner is no less brutal than our Gaucho writers. True, but his brutality is of the hallucinatory sort—the infernal, not the terrestrial sort of brutality. It is the kind that issues from dreams, the kind inaugurated by Hawthorne.

Hawthorne died on May 18, 1864, in the mountains of New Hampshire. His death was tranquil and it was mysterious, because it occurred in his sleep. Nothing keeps us from imagining that he died while dreaming and we can even invent the story that he dreamed—the last of an infinite series—and the manner in which death completed or erased it. Perhaps I shall write it some day; I shall try to redeem this deficient and too digressive essay with an acceptable story.

Van Wyck Brooks in *The Flowering of New England*, D. H. Lawrence in *Studies in Classic American Literature*, and Ludwig Lewisohn in *Story of American Literature* analyze and evaluate the work of Hawthorne. There are many biographies. I have used the one Henry James wrote in 1879 for the English Men of Letters Series.

When Hawthorne died, the other writers inherited his task of dreaming. At some future time we shall study, if your indulgence permits, the glory and the torment of Poe, in whom the dream was exalted to a nightmare.

Note on Walt Whitman

"The whole of Whitman's work is deliberate."
R. L. Stevenson, *Familiar
Studies of Men and Books* (1882)

The practice of literature sometimes fosters the ambition to construct an absolute book, a book of books that includes all the others like a Platonic archetype, an object whose virtue is not lessened by the years. Those who cherished that ambition have chosen lofty subjects: Apollonius of Rhodes, the first ship that braved the dangers of the deep; Lucan, the struggle between Caesar and Pompey, when the eagles waged war against the eagles; Camoëns, the Portuguese armies in the Orient; Donne, the circle of a soul's transmigrations according to Pythagorean dogma; Milton, the most ancient of sins and Paradise; Firdusi, the thrones of the Sassanidae. Góngora, I believe, was the first to say that an important book can exist without an important theme; the vague story told by the *Soledades* is deliberately trite, according to the observation and reproof of Cascales and Gracián (*Cartas filológicas*, VIII; *El Criticón*, II, 4). Trivial themes did not suffice for Mallarmé; he sought negative ones—the absence of a flower or a woman, the whiteness of the piece of paper before the poem. Like Pater, he felt that all the arts gravitate toward music, the

66

art that has form as its substance; his decorous profession of faith *Tout aboutit à un livre* seems to summarize the Homeric axiom that the gods fabricate misfortunes so that future generations will have something to sing about (*Odyssey*, VIII). Around 1900 Yeats searched for the absolute in the manipulation of symbols that would awaken the generic memory, or Great Memory, which pulsates beneath individual minds; those symbols could be compared to the later archetypes of Jung. Barbusse, in *L'Enfer*, a book that has been unjustly neglected, avoided (tried to avoid) the limitations of time by means of the poetical account of man's basic acts. In *Finnegans Wake* Joyce tried to achieve the same objective by the simultaneous presentation of the characteristics of different epochs. The deliberate manipulation of anachronisms to produce an appearance of eternity has also been practiced by Pound and T. S. Eliot.

I have recalled some procedures; none is more curious than the one used by Whitman in 1855. Before considering it, I should like to quote some opinions that more or less prefigure what I am going to say. The first is from the English poet Lascelles Abercrombie, who wrote that Whitman extracted from his noble experience the vivid and personal figure who is one of the few great things in modern literature: the figure of himself. The second is from Sir Edmund Gosse, who said there was no real Walt Whitman, but that Whitman was literature in the protoplasmic state: an intellectual organism that was so simple it only reflected those who approached it. The third one is mine; it is found on page 70 of the book *Discusión* (1932):

Almost everything that has been written about Whitman is falsified by two persistent errors. One is the summary identification of Whitman, the man of letters, with Whitman, the semidivine hero of *Leaves of Grass*, as Don Quixote is the hero of the *Quixote*. The other is the senseless adoption of the style and vocabulary of his poems by those who write about him, that is to say, the adoption of the same surprising phenomenon one wishes to explain.

Imagine that a biography of Ulysses (based on the testimonies of Agamemnon, Laertes, Polyphemus, Calypso, Penelope, Telemachus, the swineherd, Scylla, and Charybdis) indicated that he never left Ithaca. Such a book is fortunately hypothetical, but its particular brand of deception would be the same as the deception in all the biographies of Whitman. To progress from the paradisiacal sphere of his verses to the insipid chronicle of his days is a melancholy transition. Paradoxically, that inevitable melancholy is aggravated when the biographer chooses to overlook the fact that there are two Whitmans: the "friendly and eloquent savage" of *Leaves of Grass* and the poor writer who invented him.[1] The latter was never in California or in Platte Canyon; the former improvises an apostrophe in Platte Canyon ("Spirit that Formed this Scene") and was a miner in California ("Starting from Paumanok," 1). In 1859 the latter was in New York; on December second of that year the former was present at the execution of the old abolitionist, John Brown, in Virginia ("Year of Meteors"). The latter was born on Long Island; so was the former ("Starting from Paumanok," 1), but he was also born in one of the southern states ("Longings for Home"). The latter was chaste, reserved, and somewhat taciturn; the former, effusive and orgiastic. It is easy to multiply such contradictions; but it is more important to understand that the mere happy vagabond proposed by the verses of *Leaves of Grass* would have been incapable of writing them.

Byron and Baudelaire dramatized their unhappiness in famous volumes; Whitman, his joy. (Thirty years later, in Sils-Maria, Nietzsche would discover Zarathustra; that pedagogue is happy or, at any rate, he recommends happiness, but his principal defect is that he does not exist.) Other romantic heroes—Vathek is the first of the series, Edmond Teste is not the last—tediously emphasize their differences; Whitman, with impetuous humility, yearns to be like all men. He says that *Leaves of Grass* "is the song of a great collective, popular individual, man or woman" (*Complete Writings*, V, 192). Or in these immortal words ("Song of Myself," 17):

> These are really the thoughts of all men in all ages and lands,
>   they are not original with me,
> If they are not yours as much as mine they are nothing, or next
>   to nothing,

[1] Henry Seidel Canby (*Walt Whitman* [1943]) and Mark Van Doren in the Viking Press Anthology (1945) recognize that difference very well, but, to my knowledge, they are the only ones who do.

68

If they are not the riddle and the untying of the riddle they are
    nothing,
If they are not just as close as they are distant they are nothing.

This is the grass that grows wherever the land is and the water is,
This is the common air that bathes the globe.

Pantheism has disseminated a variety of phrases which declare that
God is several contradictory or (even better) miscellaneous things.
The prototype of such phrases is this: "I am the rite, I am the offer-
ing, I am the oblation to the parents, I am the grass, I am the prayer,
I am the libation of butter, I am the fire" (*Bhagavad-Gita*, IX, 16).
Earlier, but ambiguous, is Fragment 67 of Heraclitus: "God is day
and night, winter and summer, war and peace, satiety and hunger."
Plotinus describes for his pupils an inconceivable sky, in which "everything is everywhere, anything is all things, the sun is all the stars,
and each star is all the stars and the sun" (*Enneads*, V, 8, 4). Attar,
a twelfth-century Persian, sings of the arduous pilgrimage of the birds
in search of their king, the Simurg; many of them perish in the seas,
but the survivors discover that they are the Simurg and that the
Simurg is each one of them and all of them. Extension of the principle
of identity seems to have infinite rhetorical possibilities. Emerson, a
reader of the Hindus and of Attar, leaves us the poem "Brahma";
perhaps the most memorable of its sixteen verses is this one: "When
me they fly, I am the wings." Similar but more fundamental is "Ich
bin der Eine und bin Beide," by Stefan George (*Der Stern des
Bundes*). Walt Whitman renovated that procedure. He did not use it,
as others had, to define the divinity or to play with the "sympathies
and differences" of words; he wanted to identify himself, in a sort of
ferocious tenderness, with all men. He said ("Crossing Brooklyn
Ferry," 6):

[I] Was wayward, vain, greedy, shallow, sly, cowardly, malignant,
The wolf, the snake, the hog, not wanting in me,

And also, ("Song of Myself," 33):

I am the man, I suffer'd, I was there.
The disdain and calmness of martyrs,

The mother of old, condemn'd for a witch, burnt with dry
    wood, her children gazing on,
The hounded slave that flags in the race, leans by the fence,
    blowing, cover'd with sweat,
The twinges that sting like needles his legs and neck, the
    murderous buckshot and the bullets,
All these I feel or am.

Whitman felt and was all of them, but fundamentally he was—not
in mere history, in myth—what these two lines denote ("Song of
Myself," 24):

Walt Whitman, a kosmos, of Manhattan the son,
Turbulent, fleshy, sensual, eating, drinking, and breeding,

He was also the one he would be in the future, in our future nostalgia, which is created by these prophecies that announced it ("Full
of Life Now"):

Full of life now, compact, visible,
I, forty years old the eighty-third year of the States,
To one a century hence or any number of centuries hence,
To you yet unborn these, seeking you.

When you read these I that was visible am become invisible,
Now it is you, compact, visible, realising my poems,
    seeking me,
Fancying how happy you were if I could be with you and
    become your comrade;
Be it as if I were with you. (Be not too certain but I am
    now with you.)

Or ("Songs of Parting," 4, 5):

Camerado, this is no book,
Who touches this touches a man,
(Is it night? are we here together alone?)

I love you, I depart from materials,
I am as one disembodied, triumphant, dead.[2]

[2] The mechanism of these apostrophes is intricate. We are touched by the
fact that the poet was moved when he foresaw our emotion. Compare these

Walt Whitman, the man, was editor of the *Brooklyn Eagle* and read his basic ideas in the pages of Emerson, Hegel, and Volney; Walt Whitman, the poetic personage, evolved his ideas from contact with America through imaginary experiences in the bedrooms of New Orleans and on the battlefields of Georgia. That does not necessarily imply falsity. A false fact may be essentially true. It is said that Henry I of England never smiled after the death of his son; the fact, perhaps false, can be true as a symbol of the King's grief. In 1914 it was reported that the Germans had tortured and mutilated a number of Belgian hostages; the statement may have been false, but it effectively summarized the infinite and confused horrors of the invasion. Even more pardonable is the case of those who attribute a doctrine to vital experiences and not to a certain library or a certain epitome. In 1874 Nietzsche ridiculed the Pythagorean thesis that history repeats itself cyclically (*Vom Nutzen und Nachtheil der Historie*, 2); in 1881 he suddenly conceived that thesis on a path in the woods of Silvaplana (*Ecce homo*, 9). One could descend to the level of a detective and speak of plagiarism; if he were asked about it, Nietzsche would reply that the important consideration is the change an idea can cause in us, not the mere formulation of it.[3] The abstract proposition of divine unity is one thing; the flash of light that drove some Arab shepherds out of the desert and forced them into a battle that has not ended and which extended from Aquitaine to the Ganges is another. Whitman's plan was to display an ideal democrat, not to devise a theory.

Since Horace predicted his celestial metamorphosis with a Platonic or Pythagorean image, the theme of the poet's immortality has been classic in literature. Those who utilized it did so from motives of

---

lines by Flecker, addressed to the poet who will read him a thousand years later:

> O friend unseen, unborn, unknown,
> Student of our sweet English tongue,
> Read out my words at night, alone:
> I was a poet, I was young.

[3] Reason and conviction differ so much that the gravest objections to any philosophical doctrine usually pre-exist in the work that declares it. In the *Parmenides* Plato anticipates the argument of the third man which Aristotle will use to oppose him; Berkeley (*Dialogues*, 3) anticipates the refutations of Hume.

vainglory ("Not marble, nor the gilded monuments"), if not from a kind of bribery or even revenge. From his manipulation of the theme, Whitman derives a personal relationship with each future reader. He identifies himself with the reader, and converses with Whitman ("Salut au Monde!," 3):

What do you hear, Walt Whitman?

And it was thus that he became the eternal Whitman, the friend who is an old American poet of the eighteen hundreds and also his legend and also each one of us and also happiness. Vast and almost inhuman was the task, but no less important was the victory.

Valéry as a Symbol

To place Whitman's name next to Paul Valéry's is, at first glance, an arbitrary and (what is worse) a stupid thing to do. Valéry is a symbol of infinite skills but also of infinite scruples; Whitman, of an almost incoherent but titanic vocation of joy. Valéry is an illustrious personification of the labyrinths of the spirit; Whitman, of the interjections of the body. Valéry is a symbol of Europe and its delicate twilight; Whitman, of morning in America. The whole world of literature seems not to acknowledge two more antagonistic applications of the word *poet*. But one fact unites them: the work of both is less valuable as poetry than as the mark of an exemplary poet who was himself created by it. And for that reason the English poet Lascelles Abercrombie was able to praise Whitman for having created from the richness of his noble experience the vivid and personal figure who was one of the few really great things in the poetry of our time: the figure of himself. The statement is vague and superlative, but it has the singular virtue of not identifying Whitman, man of letters and disciple of Tennyson, with Whitman, semidivine hero of *Leaves of Grass*. The distinction is valid; Whitman wrote his rhapsodies in the role of an imaginary self, formed partly of himself, partly of each one of his readers. That is the reason for the contradictions which have exasperated critics; that is why he was in the habit of dating his poems in places he never saw; and that is why, on one page, he was born in a Southern state, and on another (which was the truth), on Long Island.

One of the aims of Whitman's compositions is to define a possible man—Walt Whitman—of unlimited and negligent bliss; no less hyperbolical, no less illusory, is the man defined by Valéry's compositions. Unlike Whitman, Valéry does not extol the human capacity for philanthropy, for fervor, and for joy; he extols the mental virtues. Valéry created Edmond Teste, a character who would be one of the myths of our century if all of us, secretly, did not consider him a mere *Doppelgänger* of Valéry. To us, Valéry is Edmond Teste. That is to say, Valéry is a derivation of Edgar Allan Poe's Chevalier Dupin and the inconceivable God of the theologians. And that supposition, probably, is not valid.

Yeats, Rilke, and Eliot have written verses more memorable than Valéry's; Joyce and Stefan George have made deeper modifications in their instrument (perhaps French is less modifiable than English and German); but behind the work of those eminent artisans is no personality comparable to Valéry's. That his personality may be a kind of projection of his work does not diminish the fact. The meritorious mission that Valéry performed (and continues to perform) is that he proposed lucidity to men in a basely romantic age, in the melancholy age of Nazism and dialectical materialism, the age of the augurs of Freud's doctrine and the traffickers in *surréalisme*.

At his death Paul Valéry leaves us the symbol of a man who is infinitely sensitive to every fact and for whom every act is a stimulus than can arouse an infinite series of thoughts. A man who transcends the differential traits of the ego and of whom we can say, like William Hazlitt of Shakespeare, "He is nothing in himself." A man whose admirable texts do not exhaust, or even define, his all-embracing possibilities. A man who, in a century that adores the chaotic idols of blood, earth, and passion, always preferred the lucid pleasures of thought and the secret adventures of order.

Buenos Aires, 1945

The Enigma of Edward FitzGerald

A man named Omar ben Ibrāhīm is born in Persia in the eleventh century of the Christian era (for him, that century was the fifth of the Hejira); he learns the Koran and its traditions with Hassan ben Sabbah, the future founder of the sect of the Hashishin or Assassins, and with Nizam-al-Mulk, who will be the vizir of Alp Arslan, conqueror of the Caucasus. The three friends, half in jest, swear that if fortune happens to favor one of them some day, the lucky one will not forget the others. After several years Nizam attains the dignity of a vizir; Omar asks only for a corner in the shadow of his friend's good fortune so that he may pray for his prosperity and meditate on mathematics. (Hassan requests and receives a high position and, in the end, has the vizir stabbed to death.) Omar receives an annual pension of ten thousand dinars from the treasury of Nishapur, and is able to devote his life to study. He does not believe in judicial astrology, but he cultivates astronomy, collaborates on the reform of the calendar promoted by the Sultan, and writes a famous treatise on algebra, which gives numerical solutions for first- and second-degree equations, and geometric solutions—by the intersection of conics—for third-degree equations. The arcana of numbers and stars do not exhaust his attention; in the solitude of his library he reads the texts of Plotinus, who in the vocabulary of Islam is the

75

Egyptian Plato or the Greek Master, and the fifty-odd epistles of the heretical and mystical encyclopedia of the Brethren of Purity, where it is written that the universe is an emanation of the Unity, and will return to the Unity. They call him a proselyte of Alfarabi, who believed that universal forms did not exist outside of things, and of Avicenna, who taught that the world was eternal. A certain chronicle tells us that he believes, or professes to believe, in transmigrations of the soul, from human to bestial body, and that once he spoke with a donkey as Pythagoras spoke with a dog. He is an atheist, but he knows the orthodox interpretation of the Koran's most difficult passages, because every cultivated man is a theologian, and faith is not a requisite. In the intervals between astronomy, algebra, and apologetics, Omar ben Ibrāhīm al-Khayyāmī writes compositions of four lines whose first, second, and last lines rhyme; he has been credited with five hundred of these quatrains—an exiguous number which will be unfavorable for his reputation, because in Persia (as in the Spain of Lope and Calderón) the poet must be prolific. In the year 517 of the Hejira, Omar is reading a tract entitled *The One and the Many*; he is interrupted by an indisposition or a premonition. He gets up, marks the page that his eyes will not see again, and reconciles himself with God—the God Who perhaps exists and Whose favor he has implored on the difficult pages of his algebra. He dies that same day, at the hour of sunset. Around that same time, on a northwesterly island which is unknown to the cartographers of Islam, a Saxon king who defeated a king of Norway is himself defeated by a Norman duke.

Seven centuries pass with their lights and agonies and mutations, and in England a man, FitzGerald, is born; he is less intellectual than Omar, but perhaps more sensitive and more sad. FitzGerald knows that his true destiny is literature, and he practices it with indolence and tenacity. He reads and rereads the *Quixote*, which seems to him almost the best of all books (but he does not wish to be unjust with Shakespeare and with "dear old Virgil"), and his love extends to the dictionary in which he seeks the words. He knows that every man who has any music in his soul can write verses ten or twelve times in the natural course of his life, if the stars are propitious, but he does not propose to abuse that modest privilege. He is a friend of famous persons (Tennyson, Carlyle, Dickens, Thackeray), to whom he does not feel inferior in spite of the fact that he is both modest and courteous. He has published a properly written dialogue, *Euphranor*, and mediocre versions of Calderón and the great Greek tragedians. From the study of Spanish he has progressed to the study of Persian; he has begun a translation of the *Mantiq al-Tayr*, that mystical epic about the birds who are looking for their king, the Simurg. They finally reach his palace, situated in back of seven seas, only to discover that they are the Simurg and the Simurg is all of them and each one of them. Around 1854 he borrows a manuscript collection of Omar's compositions. FitzGerald translates some into Latin and then has a prefiguring of a continuous and organic book made of the verses, with the images of the morning, the rose, and the nightingale at the beginning, and those of the night and the tomb at the end. FitzGerald dedicates his life of an indolent, mad, and solitary man to this improbable and even unbelievable purpose. In 1859 he publishes a first version of the *Rubáiyát*, which is followed by others, rich in variations and scruples. A miracle happens: from the fortuitous conjunction of a Persian astronomer who condescends to write poetry, and an eccentric Englishman who peruses Oriental and Hispanic books, perhaps without completely understanding them, emerges an extraordinary poet who does not resemble either of them. Swinburne writes that FitzGerald has given Omar Khayyām a perpetual place among the greatest poets of England, and Chesterton, sensitive to the romantic and classic aspects of this peerless book, observes that it has both an elusive melody and an enduring inscription. Some critics believe that FitzGerald's *Omar* is, actually, an English poem with Persian allusions; FitzGerald interpolated, refined, and invented, but his *Rubáiyát* seem to demand that we read them as Persian and ancient.

The case invites conjectures of a metaphysical nature. Omar professed (we know) the Platonic and Pythagorean doctrine of the soul's passage through many bodies; centuries later his soul may have been reincarnated in England to fulfill the literary destiny repressed by mathematics in Nishapur, in a distant Germanic language variegated with Latin. Isaac Luria the Lion taught that the soul of a dead man can enter an unhappy soul to sustain or instruct it; perhaps the soul of Omar lodged in FitzGerald's around 1857. In the *Rubáiyát* we read that universal history is a spectacle that God conceives, repre-

77

sents, and contemplates; that speculation (its technical name is pantheism) would permit us to think that the Englishman could have re-created the Persian, because both were, essentially, God—or momentary faces of God. The supposition of a beneficent chance is more credible and no less marvelous than those conjectures of a supernatural sort. Sometimes clouds form the shapes of mountains or lions; Edward FitzGerald's unhappiness and a manuscript of yellow paper with purple letters, forgotten on a shelf of the Bodleian at Oxford, formed the poem for our benefit.

All collaboration is mysterious. That by the Englishman and the Persian was more mysterious than any because the two were very different and perhaps in life they would not have become friends; death and vicissitudes and time caused one to know of the other and made them into a single poet.

About Oscar Wilde

To mention Wilde's name is to mention a dandy who was also a poet; it is to evoke the image of a gentleman dedicated to the paltry aim of startling people by his cravats and his metaphors. It is also to evoke the notion of art as a select or secret game—like the work of Hugh Vereker and Stefan George—and the poet as an industrious *monstrorum artifex* (Pliny, XXVIII, 2). It is to evoke the weary twilight of the nineteenth century and the oppressive pomp one associates with a conservatory or a masquerade ball. None of these evocations is false, but I maintain that they all correspond to partial truths and contradict, or overlook, well-known facts.

For example, consider the notion that Wilde was a kind of symbolist. A great many facts support it: around 1881 Wilde directed the Aesthetes and ten years later, the Decadents; Rebecca West falsely accuses him (*Henry James*, III) of imposing the stamp of the middle class on the Decadents; the vocabulary of the poem "The Sphinx" is studiously magnificent; Wilde was a friend of Schwob and of Mallarmé. But one important fact refutes this notion: in verse or in prose Wilde's syntax is always very simple. Of the many British writers, none is so accessible to foreigners. Readers who are incapable of deciphering a paragraph by Kipling or a stanza by William Morris begin and end *Lady Windermere's Fan* on the same afternoon. Wilde's metrical system is spontaneous or simulates spontaneity; his work does not include a single experimental verse, like this solid and wise Alexandrine by Lionel Johnson:

Alone with Christ, desolate else, left by mankind.

Wilde's technical insignificance can be an argument in favor of his intrinsic greatness. If his work corresponded to the sort of reputation he had, it would consist merely of artifices like *Les Palais Nomades* or *Los crepúsculos del jardín*, which abound in Wilde—remember Chapter XI of *Dorian Gray* or "The Harlot's House" or "Symphony in Yellow"—but his use of adjectives gave him a certain notoriety. Wilde can dispense with those purple patches—a phrase attributed to him by Ricketts and Hesketh Pearson, but which had already appeared elsewhere earlier. The fact that it was attributed to Wilde confirms the custom of linking his name to decorative passages.

Reading and rereading Wilde through the years, I notice something that his panegyrists do not seem to have even suspected: the provable and elementary fact that Wilde is almost always right. *The Soul of Man under Socialism* is not only eloquent; it is just. The miscellaneous notes that he lavished on the *Pall Mall Gazette* and the *Speaker* are filled with perspicuous observations that exceed the optimum possibilities of Leslie Stephen or Saintsbury. Wilde has been accused of practicing a kind of combinatorial art, in the manner of Raymond Lully; that is perhaps true of some of his jokes ("one of those British faces that, once seen, are always forgotten"), but not of the belief that music reveals to us an unknown and perhaps real past (*The Critic as Artist*), or that all men kill the thing they love (*The Ballad of Reading Gaol*), or that to be repentant for an act is to modify the past (*De Profundis*), or that (and this is a belief not unworthy of Léon Bloy or Swedenborg) there is no man who is not, at each moment, what he has been and what he will be (*ibid.*).[1] I do not say this to encourage my readers to venerate Wilde; but rather to indicate a mentality that is quite unlike the one generally attributed to Wilde.

[1] Compare the curious thesis of Leibnitz, which seemed so scandalous to Arnauld: "The notion of each individual includes *a priori* all the events that will happen to him." According to this dialectical fatalism, the fact that Alexander the Great would die in Babylon is a quality of that king, like arrogance.

If I am not mistaken, he was much more than an Irish Moréas; he was a man of the eighteenth century who sometimes condescended to play the game of symbolism. Like Gibbon, like Johnson, like Voltaire, he was an ingenious man who was also right. He was "remarkable for the rapidity with which he could utter fatal words."[2] He gave the century what the century demanded—*comédies larmoyantes* for the many and verbal arabesques for the few—and he executed those dissimilar things with a kind of negligent glee. His perfection has been a disadvantage; his work is so harmonious that it may seem inevitable and even trite. It is hard for us to imagine the universe without Wilde's epigrams; but that difficulty does not make them less plausible.

An aside: Oscar Wilde's name is linked to the cities of the plain; his fame, to condemnation and jail. Nevertheless (this has been perceived very clearly by Hesketh Pearson) the fundamental spirit of his work is joy. On the other hand, the powerful work of Chesterton, the prototype of physical and moral sanity, is always on the verge of becoming a nightmare. The diabolical and the horrible lie in wait on his pages; the most innocuous subject can assume the forms of terror. Chesterton is a man who wants to regain childhood; Wilde, a man who keeps an invulnerable innocence in spite of the habits of evil and misfortune.

Like Chesterton, like Lang, like Boswell, Wilde is among those fortunate writers who can do without the approval of the critics and even, at times, without the reader's approval, and the pleasure we derive from his company is irresistible and constant.

1946

[2] This sentence is by Reyes, who applies it to the Mexican male (*Reloj de sol*, p. 158).

On Chesterton

Because He does not take away
The terror from the tree . . .

Chesterton: *A Second Childhood*

Edgar Allan Poe wrote stories of pure fantastic horror or pure *bizarrerie*; he invented the detective story. That is no less certain than the fact that he did not combine the two genres. He did not inflict on C. Auguste Dupin the task of solving the ancient crime of the Man of the Crowd or of explaining the image that terrified the masked Prince Prospero in the chamber of black and scarlet. On the other hand, Chesterton lavished such *tours de force* with passion and joy. Each story in the Father Brown Saga presents a mystery, proposes explanations of a demoniacal or magical sort, and then replaces them at the end with solutions of this world. Skill is not the only virtue of those brief bits of fiction; I believe I can perceive in them an abbreviation of Chesterton's life, a symbol or reflection of Chesterton. The repetition of his formula through the years and through the books (*The Man Who Knew Too Much, The Poet and the Lunatics, The Paradoxes of Mr. Pond*) seems to confirm that this is an essential form, not a rhetorical artifice. These notes are an attempt to interpret that form.

82

But first we must reconsider some facts that are perhaps too well known. Chesterton was a Catholic, he believed in the Middle Ages of the Pre-Raphaelites ("Of London, small and white, and clean"). Like Whitman, Chesterton thought that the mere fact of existing is so prodigious that no misfortune should exempt us from a kind of cosmic gratitude. That may be a just belief, but it arouses only limited interest; to suppose that it is all Chesterton offers is to forget that a creed is the underlying factor in a series of mental and emotional processes and that a man is the whole series. In Argentina, Catholics exalt Chesterton, freethinkers reject him. Like every writer who professes a creed, Chesterton is judged by it, is condemned or acclaimed because of it. His case is not unlike that of Kipling, who is always judged with reference to the English Empire.

Poe and Baudelaire proposed the creation of a world of terror, as did Blake's tormented Urizen; it is natural for their work to teem with the forms of horror. In my opinion, Chesterton would not have tolerated the imputation of being a contriver of nightmares, a *monstrorum artifex* (Pliny, XXVIII, 2), but he tends inevitably to revert to atrocious observations. He asks if perchance a man has three eyes, or a bird three wings; in opposition to the pantheists, he speaks of a man who dies and discovers in paradise that the spirits of the angelic choirs have, every one of them, the same face he has;[1] he speaks of a jail of mirrors; of a labyrinth without a center; of a man devoured by metal automatons; of a tree that devours birds and then grows feathers instead of leaves; he imagines (*The Man Who Was Thursday*, VI) "that if a man went westward to the end of the world he would find something—say a tree—that was more or less than a tree, a tree possessed by a spirit; and that if he went east to the end of the world he would find something else that was not wholly itself—a tower, perhaps, of which the very shape was wicked." He defines the near by the far, and even by the atrocious; if he speaks of eyes, he uses the

---

[1] Amplifying a thought of Attar ("Everywhere we see only Thy face"), Jalal-uddin Rumí composed some verses that have been translated by Rückert (*Werke*, IV, 222), which state that in the heavens, in the sea, and in dreams there is One Alone; that Being is praised for having reduced to oneness the four spirited animals (earth, fire, air, and water) that draw the cart of the worlds.

words of Ezekiel (1:22) "the terrible crystal"; if of the night, he perfects an ancient horror (Apocalypse 4:6) and calls it a "monster made of eyes." Equally illustrative is the tale *How I Found the Superman*. Chesterton speaks to the Superman's parents; when he asks them what the child, who never leaves a dark room, looks like, they remind him that the Superman creates his own law and must be measured by it. On that plane he is more handsome than Apollo; but viewed from the lower plane of the average man, of course—Then they admit that it is not easy to shake hands with him, because of the difference in structure. Indeed, they are not able to state with precision whether he has hair or feathers. After a current of air kills him, several men carry away a coffin that is not of human shape. Chesterton relates this teratological fantasy as a joke.

These examples, which could easily be multiplied, prove that Chesterton restrained himself from being Edgar Allan Poe or Franz Kafka, but something in the makeup of his personality leaned toward the nightmarish, something secret, and blind, and central. Not in vain did he dedicate his first works to the justification of two great gothic craftsmen, Browning and Dickens; not in vain did he repeat that the best book to come out of Germany was *Grimm's Fairy Tales*. He reviled Ibsen and defended Rostand (perhaps indefensibly), but the Trolls and the creator of *Peer Gynt* were the stuff his dreams were made of. That discord, that precarious subjection of a demoniacal will, defines Chesterton's nature. For me, the emblems of that struggle are the adventures of Father Brown, each of which undertakes to explain an inexplicable event by reason alone.[2] That is why I said, in the first paragraph of this essay, that those stories were the key to Chesterton, the symbols and reflections of Chesterton. That is all, except that the "reason" to which Chesterton subjected his imaginings was not precisely reason but the Catholic faith or rather a collection of Hebrew imaginings that had been subjected to Plato and Aristotle.

I remember two opposing parables. The first one is from the first volume of Kafka's works. It is the story of the man who asks to be

---

[2] Most writers of detective stories usually undertake to explain the obscure rather than the inexplicable.

admitted to the law. The guardian of the first door says that there are many other doors within,[3] and that every room is under the watchful eye of a guardian, each of whom is stronger than the one before. The man sits down to wait. Days and years go by, and the man dies. In his agony he asks, "Is it possible that during the years I have been waiting, no one has wanted to enter but me?" The guardian answers, "No one has wanted to enter this door because it was destined for you alone. Now I shall close it." (In the ninth chapter of *The Trial* Kafka comments on this parable, making it even more complicated.) The other parable is in Bunyan's *Pilgrim's Progress*. People gaze enviously at a castle guarded by many warriors; a guardian at the door holds a book in which he will write the name of the one who is worthy of entering. An intrepid man approaches the guardian and says, "Write my name, sir." Then he takes out his sword and lunges at the warriors; there is an exchange of bloody blows; he forces his way through the tumult and enters the castle.

Chesterton devoted his life to the writing of the second parable, but something within him always tended to write the first.

---

[3] The notion of doors behind doors interposed between the sinner and glory is found in the *Zohar*. See Glatzer, *In Time and Eternity*, 30; also Martin Buber, *Tales of the Hasidim*, 92.

The First Wells

Harris relates that when Oscar Wilde was asked about Wells, he called him "a scientific Jules Verne." That was in 1899; it appears that Wilde thought less of defining Wells, or of annihilating him, than of changing the subject. Now the names H. G. Wells and Jules Verne have come to be incompatible. We all feel that this is true, but still it may be well to examine the intricate reasons on which our feeling is based.

The most obvious reason is a technical one. Before Wells resigned himself to the role of a sociological spectator, he was an admirable storyteller, an heir to the concise style of Swift and Edgar Allan Poe; Verne was a pleasant and industrious journeyman. Verne wrote for adolescents; Wells, for all ages. There is another difference, which Wells himself once indicated: Verne's stories deal with probable things (a submarine, a ship larger than those existing in 1872, the discovery of the South Pole, the talking picture, the crossing of Africa in a balloon, the craters of an extinguished volcano that lead to the center of the earth); the short stories Wells wrote concern mere possibilities, if not impossible things (an invisible man, a flower that devours a man, a crystal egg that reflects the events on Mars, a man who returns from the future with a flower of the future, a man who returns from the other life with his heart on the right side, because he has been completely inverted, as in a mirror). I have read that Verne, scandalized by the license permitted by *The First Men in the Moon*, exclaimed indignantly, "*Il invente!*"

The reasons I have given seem valid enough, but they do not explain why Wells is infinitely superior to the author of *Hector Servadac*, and also to Rosney, Lytton, Robert Paltock, Cyrano, or any other precursor of his methods.[1] Even his best plots do not adequately solve the problem. In long books the plot can be only a pretext, or a point of departure. It is important for the composition of the work, but not for the reader's enjoyment of it. That is true of all genres; the best detective stories are not those with the best plots. (If plots were everything, the *Quixote* would not exist and Shaw would be inferior to O'Neill.) In my opinion, the excellence of Wells's first novels—*The Island of Dr. Moreau*, for example, or *The Invisible Man*—has a deeper origin. Not only do they tell an ingenious story; but they tell a story symbolic of processes that are somehow inherent in all human destinies. The harassed invisible man who has to sleep as though his eyes were wide open because his eyelids do not exclude light is our solitude and our terror; the conventicle of seated monsters who mouth a servile creed in their night is the Vatican and is Lhasa. Work that endures is always capable of an infinite and plastic ambiguity; it is all things for all men, like the Apostle; it is a mirror that reflects the reader's own traits and it is also a map of the world. And it must be ambiguous in an evanescent and modest way, almost in spite of the author; he must appear to be ignorant of all symbolism. Wells displayed that lucid innocence in his first fantastic exercises, which are to me the most admirable part of his admirable work.

Those who say that art should not propagate doctrines usually refer to doctrines that are opposed to their own. Naturally this is not my own case; I gratefully profess almost all the doctrines of Wells, but I deplore his inserting them into his narratives. An heir of the British nominalists, Wells condemns our custom of speaking of the "tenacity of England" or the "intrigues of Prussia." The arguments against that harmful mythology seem to be irreproachable, but not

---

[1] In *The Outline of History* (1931) Wells praises the work of two other precursors: Francis Bacon and Lucian of Samosata.

the fact of interpolating them into the story of Mr. Parham's dream. As long as an author merely relates events or traces the slight deviations of a conscience, we can suppose him to be omniscient, we can confuse him with the universe or with God; but when he descends to the level of pure reason, we know he is fallible. Reality is inferred from events, not reasonings; we permit God to affirm *I am that I am* (Exodus 3:14), not to declare and analyze, like Hegel or Anselm, the *argumentum ontologicum*. God must not theologize; the writer must not invalidate with human arguments the momentary faith that art demands of us. There is another consideration: the author who shows aversion to a character seems not to understand him completely, seems to confess that the character is not inevitable for him. We distrust his intelligence, as we would distrust the intelligence of a God who maintained heavens and hells. God, Spinoza has written, does not hate anyone and does not love anyone (*Ethics*, 5, 17).

Like Quevedo, like Voltaire, like Goethe, like some others, Wells is less a man of letters than a literature. He wrote garrulous books in which the gigantic felicity of Charles Dickens somehow reappears; he bestowed sociological parables with a lavish hand; he constructed encyclopedias, enlarged the possibilities of the novel, rewrote the Book of Job—"that great Hebrew imitation of the Platonic dialogue"; for our time, he wrote a very delightful autobiography without pride and without humility; he combated communism, Nazism, and Christianity; he debated (politely and mortally) with Belloc; he chronicled the past, chronicled the future, recorded real and imaginary lives. Of the vast and diversified library he left us, nothing has pleased me more than his narration of some atrocious miracles: *The Time Machine, The Island of Dr. Moreau, The Plattner Story, The First Men in the Moon.* They are the first books I read; perhaps they will be the last. I think they will be incorporated, like the fables of Theseus or Ahasuerus, into the general memory of the species and even transcend the fame of their creator or the extinction of the language in which they were written.

The *Biathanatos*

To De Quincey (my debt to him is so vast that to specify a part of it seems to repudiate or to silence the others) I owe my first knowledge of the *Biathanatos*. It was written at the beginning of the seventeenth century by the great poet John Donne,[1] who left the manuscript to Sir Robert Carr with one stipulation: that it be published or burned. Donne died in 1631; civil war broke out in 1642; in 1644 the poet's eldest son published the old manuscript to save it from burning. The *Biathanatos* is about two hundred pages long; De Quincey (*Writings*, VIII, 336) sums them up as follows: Suicide is one form of homicide; the canonists distinguish voluntary homicide from justifiable homicide; logically, that distinction should also apply to suicide. As not every murderer is an assassin, not every self-murderer is guilty of mortal sin. This is the apparent thesis of the *Biathanatos*; it is stated in the subtitle (*That Self-homicide is not so naturally Sin that it may never be otherwise*), and it is illustrated,

---

[1] His greatness as a poet can be shown by these verses:

> Licence my roving hands and let them go
> Before, behind, between, above, below.
> O my America! my new-found-land. . . .
> (Elegies, XIX)

or burdened, by a learned catalogue of fabulous or authentic examples: Homer,[2] who had written a thousand things that no one else could understand, and who was said to have hanged himself because he did not understand the riddle of the fishermen; the pelican, symbol of paternal love; and the bees which, as the *Hexameron* of Ambrose declares, kill themselves when they have violated the laws of their king. The catalogue fills three pages and I have observed that it has this show of vanity: it includes obscure examples (Festus, favorite of Domitian, who killed himself to conceal the ravages of a skin disease), and omits others of equally persuasive virtue—Seneca, Themistocles, Cato—which could have seemed too easy.

Epictetus ("Remember the essential thing: the door is open") and Schopenhauer ("Is Hamlet's soliloquy the meditation of a criminal?") have written many pages to vindicate suicide; our inner certainty that those defenders are right causes us to read them carelessly. That is what happened to me with the *Biathanatos* until I noticed, or thought I noticed, an implicit or esoteric plot beneath the apparent one.

We shall never know whether Donne wrote the *Biathanatos* with the deliberate aim of insinuating that hidden plot or whether a prefiguring of that plot, even if only momentary or crepuscular, called him to the task. I think the second theory is the more probable one; the hypothesis of a book that says *B* in order to say *A*, as in a cryptogram, is artificial, but the thought of a work inspired by an imperfect intuition is not. Hugh Fausset has suggested that Donne planned to culminate his vindication of suicide with suicide. That Donne may have played with such an idea is possible or even probable; that Fausset's suggestion is sufficient to explain the *Biathanatos* is, naturally, ridiculous.

In the third part of the *Biathanatos* Donne considers the voluntary deaths recorded by the Scriptures; to no other does he devote as many pages as to the death of Samson. He begins by establishing that this "exemplary man" is the emblem of Christ and that to the Greeks he seems to have been the archetype of Hercules. Francisco de Vi-

[2] Compare the sepulchral epigram of Alcaeus of Messene (*Greek Anthology*, VII, I).

toria and the Jesuit Gregorio de Valencia did not wish to include him among the suicides. To refute them, Donne quotes the last words Samson said before he wreaked his vengeance: "Let me die with the Philistines" (Judges 16:30). He also refutes the conjecture of St. Augustine, who affirms that in breaking the pillars of the temple Samson was not guilty of the deaths of others or of his own death, but was obeying an inspiration of the Holy Spirit, "like the sword whose blade is guided by the will of the user" (*The City of God* I, 20). After proving that this conjecture is unfounded, Donne closes the chapter with a line by Benito Pererio, which states that Samson, no less in his death than in other acts, was the symbol of Christ.

Inverting the Augustinian thesis, the quietists believed that Samson "killed himself with the Philistines because of the violence of the devil" (*Heterodox Spaniards*, V, 1, 8); Milton (*Samson Agonistes*) vindicated him from the attribution of suicide; Donne, I suspect, saw nothing in that casuistical problem except a sort of metaphor or image. Samson's case did not matter to him—and indeed, why should it—or it mattered only, we shall say, as an "emblem of Christ." Nearly all Old Testament heroes have received that distinction: for St. Paul, Adam is the figure of the One Who was to come; for St. Augustine, Abel represents the Saviour's death, and his brother Seth, the resurrection; for Quevedo, "Job was a prodigious outline of Christ." Donne made use of that trivial analogy to show his reader that it might well be false when said of Samson, but that it was not when said of Christ.

The chapter that speaks directly of Christ is not effusive. It merely invokes two scriptural passages: the phrase "I lay down my life for the sheep" (John 10:15) and the curious expression "he gave up the ghost," which the four Evangelists use to say "died." From those passages, which are confirmed by the verse "No man taketh my life from me, but I lay it down of myself" (John 10:18), Donne infers that the suffering on the Cross did not kill Jesus Christ but that He, in fact, killed Himself with a prodigious and voluntary emission of His soul. Donne wrote that conjecture down in 1608; in 1631 he included it in a sermon he preached, at the point of death, in the chapel of Whitehall Palace.

The avowed purpose of the *Biathanatos* is to palliate suicide; the underlying aim is to indicate that Christ committed suicide.[3] It seems unlikely and even incredible that Donne's only way to reveal this thesis was the use of a verse from St. John and the repetition of the verb *to expire*; no doubt he preferred not to insist on a blasphemous theme. For the Christian the life and death of Christ are the central occurrences in the history of the world. The previous ages prepared the way for those events, and the subsequent centuries reflected them. Before Adam was formed from the dust of the earth, before the firmament separated the waters from the waters, the Father already knew that the Son would die on the Cross, and He created the earth and the heavens as a stage for the Son's future death. Christ died a voluntary death, Donne suggests, implying that the elements and the world and the generations of men and Egypt and Rome and Babylon and Judah were drawn from nothingness to destroy Him. Perhaps iron was created for the nails, thorns for the crown of mockery, and blood and water for the wound. That baroque idea is perceived beneath the *Biathanatos*—the idea of a god who fabricates the universe in order to fabricate his scaffold.

As I reread this essay, I think of the tragic Philipp Batz, who is called Philipp Mainländer in the history of philosophy. Like me, he was an impassioned reader of Schopenhauer, under whose influence (and perhaps under the influence of the Gnostics) he imagined that we are fragments of a God who destroyed Himself at the beginning of time, because He did not wish to exist. Universal history is the obscure agony of those fragments. Mainländer was born in 1841; in 1876 he published his book *Philosophy of the Redemption*. That same year he killed himself.

[3] Cf. De Quincey, *Writings*, VIII, 398; Kant, *Religion innerhalb der Grenzen der Vernunft*, II, 2.

Pascal

My friends tell me that the thoughts of Pascal help them to think. Certainly there is nothing in the universe that does not serve as a stimulus to thought; but I have never seen in those memorable fragments a contribution to the problems, illusory or real, they undertake to solve. I have seen them instead as predicates of the subject Pascal, as traits or epithets of Pascal. Just as the definition "quintessence of dust" does not help us to understand men but to understand Prince Hamlet, so the definition *"roseau pensant"* does not help us to understand men but to understand one man, Pascal.

Valéry, I believe, accuses Pascal of voluntary dramatization; the fact is that his book does not project the image of a doctrine or a dialectical process but of a poet lost in time and space. In time, because if the future and the past are infinite, there will not really be a when; in space, because if every being is equidistant from the infinite and the infinitesimal, there will not be a where. Pascal mentions "the opinions of Copernicus" with disdain, but his work reflects the confusion of a theologian exiled from the orb of the Almagest and lost in the Copernican universe of Kepler and Bruno. Pascal's world is the world of Lucretius (and also the world of Spencer), but the infinity that enraptured the Roman awes the Frenchman. Of course the latter is looking for God, and the former proposes to free us from the fear of the gods.

Pascal, they tell us, found God, but his manifestation of that joy is less eloquent than his manifestation of solitude, in which he had no equal. Let it suffice to recall the famous Fragment 207 of the Brunschvicg edition (*Combien de royaumes nous ignorent!*) and Fragment 205, in which he speaks of "the infinite immensity of spaces I do not know *and which do not know me.*" In the first one, the vast word *royaumes* and the disdainful final verb impress one physically. Once I thought that this exclamation was of biblical origin. I remember that I perused the Scriptures; I did not find the passage I was looking for, and which perhaps does not exist, but I did find its perfect opposite—the tremulous words of a man who knows himself to be naked to his entrails under God's watchfulness. The Apostle Paul (I Corinthians 13:12) says: "For now we see through a glass, darkly; but then face to face: now I know in part; but then shall I know *even as also I am known.*"

Fragment 72 is also worthy of note. In the second paragraph Pascal asserts that nature (space) is "an infinite sphere having its center everywhere and its circumference nowhere." Pascal could have found that sphere in Rabelais (III, 13), who attributes it to Hermes Trismegistus, or in the symbolical *Roman de la Rose*, which says that it is from Plato. But that is not important; the significant thing is that the metaphor Pascal uses to define space was used by those who preceded him (and by Sir Thomas Browne in *Religio Medici*) to define the divinity.[1] The grandeur that affects Pascal is not the grandeur of the Creator, but that of the Creation.

When he speaks of disorder and misery with incorruptible words (*on mourra seul*), he is one of the most pathetic men in the history of Europe; when he applies the computation of probabilities to apolo-

[1] I do not recall that history records conical, cubical, or pyramidal gods, although it does record idols. On the other hand, the form of the sphere is perfect and corresponds to the divinity (Cicero, *De natura deorum*, II, 17). God was spherical for Xenophanes and for the poet Parmenides. In the opinion of some historians, Empedocles (Fragment 28) and Melissus conceived Him as an infinite sphere. Origen believed that the dead would return to life in the form of spheres; Fechner (*Vergleichende Anatomie der Engel*) attributed that form, which is the shape of the visual organ, to the angels.

Before Pascal, the noted pantheist Giordano Bruno applied the sentence of Trismegistus to the material universe.

94

getics, he is one of the most vain and frivolous. He is not a mystic; he belongs to those Christians, denounced by Swedenborg, who suppose that heaven is a reward and hell a punishment and who, accustomed to melancholy meditation, do not know how to speak with the angels.[2] God matters less to Pascal than the refutation of those who deny Him.

The Zacharie Tourneur edition (Paris, 1942) seeks to reproduce, by means of a complex system of typographical symbols, the "unfinished, bristly, and confused" aspect of the manuscript; it is evident that this aim has been accomplished. The notes, on the other hand, are poor. And so, on page 71 of the first volume, there is a fragment that develops the well-known cosmological proof of St. Thomas and Leibnitz in seven lines. The editor, who does not recognize it, observes: "Perhaps Pascal is making a skeptic speak here."

Following a number of the texts, the editor cites similar passages from Montaigne or the Sacred Scriptures; this work could be enlarged. For an explanation of the *Pari*, it would be appropriate to mention the texts of Arnobius, Sirmond, and Algazel that were indicated by Asín Palacios (*Huellas del Islam*, Madrid, 1941); for an explanation of the fragment against painting, that passage from the tenth book of *The Republic*, where we are told that God creates the Archetype of the table, the carpenter creates a copy of the Archetype, and the painter, a copy of the copy; for an explanation of Fragment 72 ("Je lui veux peindre l'immensité . . . dans l'enceinte de ce raccourci d'atome . . ."), its prefiguration in the concept of the microcosm, and its reappearance in Leibnitz (*Monadologie*, 67), and in Hugo ("La chauve-souris"):

> Le moindre grain de sable est un globe qui roule
> Traînant comme la terre une lugubre foule
> Qui s'abhorre et s'acharne . . .

Democritus thought the infinite yields identical worlds, in which identical men fulfill without variation identical destinies; Pascal (who also could have been influenced by the ancient words of An-

---

[2] *De Coelo et inferno*, 535. For Swedenborg, as for Boehme (*Sex puncta theosophica*, 9, 34), heaven and hell are states that man seeks freely, not penal and pious establishments. Cf. also Bernard Shaw, *Man and Superman*, III.

axagoras to the effect that everything is within each thing) included with those identical worlds some worlds inside of others, so that there is no atom in space that does not contain universes; no universe that is not also an atom. It is logical to think (although he did not say it) that he saw himself multiplied in them, endlessly.

The Meeting in a Dream

꽃 After conquering the Circles of Hell and the arduous borders
of Purgatory, Dante sees Beatrice at last in the Earthly Paradise. Ozanam conjectures that this scene (certainly one of the most
astonishing in all literature) is the primitive nucleus of the *Comedy*.
My purpose is to relate it, to repeat what the scholiasts say, and to
present an observation, perhaps new, of a psychological nature.

On the morning of April 13, 1300, the day before the last day of
his journey, Dante, his tasks accomplished, enters the Earthly Paradise, which flourishes on the summit of Purgatory. He has seen the
temporal fire and the eternal one, he has passed through a wall of
fire, his will is free and upright. Virgil has crowned and mitred him
lord of himself (*per ch'io te sovra te corono e mitrio*). He follows
the paths of the ancient garden to a river that transcends all other
waters in purity, although neither the sun nor the moon penetrates
the trees to illuminate it. Music floats on the air, and a mysterious
procession advances on the opposite bank. Twenty-four elders in
white robes and four animals, each with six wings adorned with open
eyes, precede a triumphal chariot drawn by a griffin. At the right
wheel three women are dancing; one is so ruddy that we would
scarcely be able to see her in a fire. Beside the left wheel there are
four women in purple raiment, one of whom has three eyes. The
chariot stops and a veiled woman appears; her costume is the color

97

of a living flame. Not by sight but by the stupor of his spirit and the fear in his blood, Dante knows that it is Beatrice. On the threshold of Glory he feels the love that had transfixed him so many times in Florence. Like a frightened child he looks for Virgil's protection, but Virgil is no longer beside him.

> Ma Virgilio n'avea lasciati scemi
> di sé, Virgilio dolcissimo patre,
> Virgilio a cui per mia salute die'mi.

Imperiously, Beatrice calls him by name. She tells him not to mourn Virgil's disappearance but rather his own sins. With irony she asks him how he has deigned to tread where men are happy. The air has become populated with angels; implacably, Beatrice enumerates Dante's aberrations. She says that her quest for him in dreams was unavailing; he fell so low that the only means for his salvation was to show him the reprobates. Dante lowers his eyes, mortified, and stammers and weeps. The fabulous beings listen; Beatrice obliges him to make a public confession. This, then, in imperfect prose, is the pitiful scene of the first meeting with Beatrice in Paradise. Theophil Spoerri (*Einführung in die Göttliche Komödie*, Zürich, 1946) makes this curious observation: "Undoubtedly Dante himself had imagined that meeting differently. Nothing on the previous pages indicates that the greatest humiliation of his life awaited him there."

Commentators decipher this scene figure by figure. The twenty-four elders who lead the procession (Apocalypse 4:4) are the twenty-four books of the Old Testament, according to the *Prologus Galeatus* of St. Jerome. The animals with six wings are the Evangelists (Tommaseo) or the Gospels (Lombardi). The six wings are the six laws (Pietro di Dante) or the diffusion of doctrine in the six spatial directions (Francesco da Buti). The chariot is the Universal Church; the two wheels are the two Testaments (Buti), or the active and the contemplative life (Benvenuto da Imola), or St. Dominic and St. Francis (*Paradiso*, XII, 106–111), or Justice and Piety (Luigi Pietrobono). The griffin—lion and eagle—is Christ, by the hypostatical union of the Word with human nature: Didron maintains that it is the Pope, "who as pontiff or eagle, ascends to the throne of God to receive his orders, and as lion or king walks the earth with fortitude and vigor." The women dancing at the right wheel are the theological virtues; those dancing at the left, the cardinal ones. The woman endowed with three eyes is Prudence, which sees the past, the present, and the future. Beatrice arrives and Virgil disappears, because Virgil is reason and Beatrice faith—and also, according to Vitali, because Christian culture followed classical culture.

The interpretations I have enumerated are no doubt plausible enough. Logically (not poetically) they justify the ambiguities quite adequately. After defending some of them, Carlo Steiner writes: "A three-eyed woman is a monster, but the Poet does not bow to the restrictions of art here because he is more interested in expressing the moral code that is dear to him. This is an unequivocal proof that not art but the love of the Good occupied first place in the soul of this very great artist." Less effusively, Vitali corroborates that opinion: "The desire to allegorize leads Dante to inventions of dubious beauty."

Two facts seem to be indisputable. Dante wanted the procession to be beautiful (*Non che Roma di carro così bello Rallegrasse Affricano*); the procession is of a complicated ugliness. A griffin attached to a chariot, animals whose wings are studded with open eyes, a green woman, a crimson one, another who has three eyes, a man who walks in his sleep, all seem to belong less to Glory than to the vain Circles of Hell. Their horror is not lessened by the fact that one of those figures is from the prophetic books (*ma leggi Ezechiel che li dipigne*) and others are from the Revelation of St. John. My reproach is not an anachronism; the other scenes of Paradise exclude the monstrous.[1]

Every commentator has emphasized the severity of Beatrice, and some have stressed the ugliness of certain symbols. In my opinion, both anomalies have a common origin. Of course, this is merely a conjecture; I shall explain it briefly.

To fall in love is to create a religion that has a fallible god. That Dante professed an idolatrous adoration for Beatrice is a truth that

[1] After I had written the foregoing lines, I read in the glosses of Francesco Torraca that an Italian bestiary identifies the griffin as the symbol of the devil (*Per lo Grifone entendo lo nemico*). Shall I add that in *The Exeter Book* the panther, animal of melodious voice and soft breath, is the symbol of the Redeemer?

does not bear contradicting; that she once ridiculed him and another time rebuffed him are facts recorded by the *Vita nuova*. Some maintain that those facts are symbolic of others. If that were true, it would strengthen even more our certainty of an unhappy and superstitious love. Dante, when Beatrice was dead, when Beatrice was lost forever, played with the idea of finding her, to mitigate his sorrow. I believe that he erected the triple architecture of his poem simply to insert that encounter. Then what usually happens in dreams happened to him. In adversity we dream of good fortune, and the intimate awareness that we cannot attain it is enough to corrupt our dream, clouding it with sad restraints. That was the case with Dante. Refused forever by Beatrice, he dreamed of Beatrice, but he dreamed her very austere, but he dreamed her inaccessible, but he dreamed her in a chariot drawn by a lion that was a bird and was all bird or all lion when it was reflected in her eyes (*Purgatorio*, XXXI, 121). Those facts can be the prefiguration of a nightmare, which is set forth and described at length in the following canto. Beatrice disappears; an eagle, a vixen, and a dragon attack the chariot; the wheels and the pole are covered with feathers; then the chariot ejects seven heads (*Trasformato cosi'l dificio santo Mise fuor teste*); a giant and a harlot usurp Beatrice's place.[2]

Infinitely Beatrice existed for Dante; Dante existed very little, perhaps not at all, for Beatrice. Our piety, our veneration cause us to forget that pitiful inharmony, which was unforgettable for Dante. I read and reread about the vicissitudes of their illusory encounter, and I think of two lovers who were dreamed by Alighieri in the hurricane of the Second Circle and who are dark emblems, although he perhaps neither knew that nor intended it, of the happiness he did not attain. I think of Francesca and of Paolo, united forever in their Hell. *Questi, che mai da me non fia diviso.* With frightening love, with anxiety, with admiration, with envy, Dante must have formed that line.

---

[2] One will object that such ugliness is the reverse of the preceding "beauty." Yes, but it is significant. Allegorically, the eagle's aggression represents the first persecutions; the vixen, heresy; the dragon, Satan or Mohammed or the Antichrist; the heads, the capital sins (Benvenuto da Imola) or the sacraments (Buti); the giant, Philip IV; the harlot, the Church.

100

The Analytical Language of John Wilkins

I see that the fourteenth edition of the *Encyclopaedia Britannica* has omitted the article about John Wilkins. The omission is justified if we remember how trivial it was (twenty lines of biographical data: Wilkins was born in 1614, Wilkins died in 1672, Wilkins was the chaplain of the Prince Palatine, Charles Louis; Wilkins was appointed rector of one of the colleges of Oxford; Wilkins was the first secretary of the Royal Society of London, etc.); but not if we consider the speculative work of Wilkins. He abounded in happy curiosities: he was interested in theology, cryptography, music, the manufacture of transparent beehives, the course of an invisible planet, the possibility of a trip to the moon, the possibility and the principles of a world language. It was to this last problem that he dedicated the book *An Essay towards a Real Character and a Philosophical Language* (600 pages in quarto, 1668). Our National Library does not have a copy of that book. To write this article I have consulted *The Life and Times of John Wilkins* by P. A. Wright Henderson (1910), the *Woerterbuch der Philosophie* by Fritz Mauthner (1924), *Delphos* by E. Sylvia Pankhurst (1935), and *Dangerous Thoughts* by Lancelot Hogben (1939).

At one time or another, we have all suffered through those unappealable debates in which a lady, with copious interjections and

101

anacolutha, swears that the word *luna* is more (or less) expressive than the word *moon*. Apart from the self-evident observation that the monosyllable *moon* may be more appropriate to represent a very simple object than the disyllabic word *luna*, nothing can be contributed to such discussions. After the compound words and derivatives have been taken away, all the languages in the world (not excluding Johann Martin Schleyer's *volapük* and Peano's romance-like *interlingua*) are equally inexpressive. There is no edition of the Royal Spanish Academy *Grammar* that does not ponder "the envied treasure of picturesque, happy and expressive words in the very rich Spanish language," but that is merely an uncorroborated boast. Every few years the Royal Academy issues a dictionary to define Spanish expressions. In the universal language conceived by Wilkins around the middle of the seventeenth century each word defines itself. Descartes had already noted in a letter dated November, 1629, that by using the decimal system of numeration we could learn in a single day to name all quantities to infinity, and to write them in a new language, the language of numbers.[1] He also proposed the formation of a similar, general language that would organize and contain all human thought. Around 1664 John Wilkins began to undertake that task.

Wilkins divided the universe into forty categories or classes, which were then subdivisible into differences, subdivisible in turn into species. To each class he assigned a monosyllable of two letters; to each difference, a consonant; to each species, a vowel. For example, *de* means element; *deb*, the first of the elements, fire; *deba*, a portion of the element of fire, a flame. In a similar language invented by Letellier (1850) *a* means animal; *ab*, mammalian; *abi*, herbivorous; *abiv*, equine; *abo*, carnivorus; *aboj*, feline; *aboje*, cat; etc. In the language of Bonifacio Sotos Ochando (1845) *imaba* means building;

[1] Theoretically, the number of systems of numeration is unlimited. The most complex (for the use of divinities and angels) would record an infinite number of symbols, one for each whole number; the simplest requires only two. Zero is written 0, one 1, two 10, three 11, four 100, five 101, six 110, seven 111, eight 1000 . . . It is the invention of Leibnitz, who was apparently stimulated by the enigmatic hexagrams of the Yi tsing.

102

imaca, brothel; *imafe,* hospital; *imafo,* pesthouse; *imari,* house; *imaru,* country estate; *imede,* pillar; *imedo,* post; *imego,* floor; *imela,* ceiling; *imogo,* window; *bire,* bookbinder, *birer,* to bind books. (I found this in a book published in Buenos Aires in 1886: the *Curso de lengua universal* by Dr. Pedro Mata.)

The words of John Wilkins's analytical language are not stupid arbitrary symbols; every letter is meaningful, as the letters of the Holy Scriptures were meaningful for the cabalists. Mauthner observes that children could learn Wilkins's language without knowing that it was artificial; later, in school, they would discover that it was also a universal key and a secret encyclopedia.

After defining Wilkins's procedure, one must examine a problem that is impossible or difficult to postpone: the meaning of the fortieth table, on which the language is based. Consider the eighth category, which deals with stones. Wilkins divides them into the following classifications: ordinary (flint, gravel, slate); intermediate (marble, amber, coral); precious (pearl, opal); transparent (amethyst, sapphire); and insoluble (coal, clay, and arsenic). The ninth category is almost as alarming as the eighth. It reveals that metals can be imperfect (vermilion, quicksilver); artificial (bronze, brass); recremental (filings, rust); and natural (gold, tin, copper). The whale appears in the sixteenth category: it is a viviparous, oblong fish. These ambiguities, redundances, and deficiencies recall those attributed by Dr. Franz Kuhn to a certain Chinese encyclopedia entitled *Celestial Emporium of Benevolent Knowledge.* On those remote pages it is written that animals are divided into (a) those that belong to the Emperor, (b) embalmed ones, (c) those that are trained, (d) suckling pigs, (e) mermaids, (f) fabulous ones, (g) stray dogs, (h) those that are included in this classification, (i) those that tremble as if they were mad, (j) innumerable ones, (k) those drawn with a very fine camel's hair brush, (l) others, (m) those that have just broken a flower vase, (n) those that resemble flies from a distance. The Bibliographical Institute of Brussels also resorts to chaos: it has parceled the universe into 1,000 subdivisions: Number 262 corresponds to the Pope; Number 282, to the Roman Catholic Church; Number 263, to the Lord's Day; Number 268, to Sunday schools;

103

Number 298, to Mormonism; and Number 294, to Brahmanism, Buddhism, Shintoism, and Taoism. It also tolerates heterogeneous subdivisions, for example, Number 179: "Cruelty to animals. Protection of animals. Moral Implications of duelling and suicide. Various vices and defects. Various virtues and qualities."

I have noted the arbitrariness of Wilkins, of the unknown (or apocryphal) Chinese encyclopedist, and of the Bibliographical Institute of Brussels; obviously there is no classification of the universe that is not arbitrary and conjectural. The reason is very simple: we do not know what the universe is. "This world," wrote David Hume, ". . . was only the first rude essay of some infant deity who afterwards abandoned it, ashamed of his lame performance; it is the work only of some dependent, inferior deity, and is the object of derision to his superiors; it is the production of old age and dotage in some superannuated deity, and ever since his death has run on . . ." (*Dialogues Concerning Natural Religion*, V, 1779). We must go even further; we must suspect that there is no universe in the organic, unifying sense inherent in that ambitious word. If there is, we must conjecture its purpose; we must conjecture the words, the definitions, the etymologies, the synonymies of God's secret dictionary.

But the impossibility of penetrating the divine scheme of the universe cannot dissuade us from outlining human schemes, even though we are aware that they are provisional. Wilkins's analytical language is not the least admirable of those schemes. It is composed of classes and species that are contradictory and vague; its device of using the letters of the words to indicate divisions and subdivisions is, without a doubt, ingenious. The word *salmon* does not tell us anything about the object it represents; *zana*, the corresponding word, defines (for the person versed in the forty categories and the classes of those categories) a scaly river fish with reddish flesh. (Theoretically, a language in which the name of each being would indicate all the details of its destiny, past and future, is not inconceivable.)

Hopes and utopias aside, these words by Chesterton are perhaps the most lucid ever written about language:

Man knows that there are in the soul tints more bewildering, more numberless, and more nameless than the colours of an autumn forest; . . .

104

Yet he seriously believes that these things can every one of them, in all their tones and semi-tones, in all their blends and unions, be accurately represented by an arbitrary system of grunts and squeals. He believes that an ordinary civilized stockbroker can really produce out of his own inside noises which denote all the mysteries of memory and all the agonies of desire. (*G. F. Watts*, 1904, p. 88)

Kafka and His Precursors

Once I planned to make a survey of Kafka's precursors. At first I thought he was as singular as the fabulous Phoenix; when I knew him better I thought I recognized his voice, or his habits, in the texts of various literatures and various ages. I shall record a few of them here, in chronological order.

The first is Zeno's paradox against movement. A moving body on *A* (declares Aristotle) will not be able to reach point *B*, because before it does, it must cover half of the distance between the two, and before that, half of the half, and before that, half of the half of the half, and so on to infinity; the formula of this famous problem is, exactly, that of *The Castle;* and the moving body and the arrow and Achilles are the first Kafkian characters in literature.

In the second text that happened to come to my attention, the affinity is not of form but rather of tone. It is an apologue by Han Yu, a prose writer of the ninth century, and it is included in the admirable *Anthologie raisonnée de la littérature chinoise* by Margouliès (1948). This is the paragraph I marked, a mysterious and tranquil one:

It is universally admitted that the unicorn is a supernatural being and one of good omen; this is declared in the odes, in the annals, in the biographies of illustrious men, and in other texts of unquestioned authority. Even the women and children of the populace know that the unicorn constitutes a favorable presage. But this animal is not one of the domestic animals, it is not always easy to find, it does not lend itself to classification. It is not like the horse or the bull, the wolf or the deer. And therefore we could be in the presence of the unicorn and we would not know for certain that it was one. We know that a certain animal with a mane is a horse, and that one with horns is a bull. We do not know what the unicorn is like.[1]

The third text proceeds from a more foreseeable source: the writings of Kierkegaard. The mental affinity of both writers is known to almost everyone; what has not yet been brought out, as far as I know, is that Kierkegaard, like Kafka, abounded in religious parables on contemporary and middle-class themes. Lowrie, in his *Kierkegaard* (Oxford University Press, 1938), mentions two. One is the story of a forger who examines Bank of England notes while under constant surveillance; in the same way, God must have been suspicious of Kierkegaard and must have entrusted him with a mission simply because He knew that he was accustomed to evil. Expeditions to the North Pole are the subject of the other. Danish clergymen had announced from their pulpits that to participate in those expeditions would be beneficial for the eternal salvation of the soul. However, they admitted that it was difficult and perhaps impossible to reach the Pole, and that not everyone could undertake such an adventure. Finally, they announced that any journey—from Denmark to London, say, by ship—or a Sunday outing in a hackney coach, was in fact a real expedition to the North Pole.

The fourth prefiguration I found is the poem "Fears and Scruples," by Browning, which was published in 1876. A man has, or thinks he has, a famous friend. He has never seen this friend, and the latter has not yet been able to help him, but he is reputed to have very noble qualities, and letters he has written are circulated. Some question his good qualities, and handwriting experts assert that the letters are apocryphal. In the last verse the man asks: "What if this friend happen to be—God?"

[1] The failure to recognize the sacred animal and its opprobrious or casual death at the hands of the populace are traditional themes in Chinese literature. See the last chapter of Jung's *Psychologie und Alchemie* (Zürich, 1944), which includes two curious illustrations.

107

My notes also include two short stories. One is from the *Histoires désobligeantes*, by Léon Bloy, and tells of people who have a collection of atlases, globes, train schedules, and trunks, and then die without ever having left the town where they were born. The other is entitled "Carcassonne" and is by Lord Dunsany. An invincible army of warriors departs from an enormous castle, subjugates kingdoms, sees monsters, conquers deserts and mountains, but never arrives at Carcassonne, although the men catch sight of the city once from afar. (This story is the exact opposite of the other one; in the first story, a city is never departed from; in the second, a city is never reached.)

If I am not mistaken, the heterogeneous selections I have mentioned resemble Kafka's work: if I am not mistaken, not all of them resemble each other, and this fact is the significant one. Kafka's idiosyncrasy, in greater or lesser degree, is present in each of these writings, but if Kafka had not written we would not perceive it; that is to say, it would not exist. The poem "Fears and Scruples" by Robert Browning is like a prophecy of Kafka's stories, but our reading of Kafka refines and changes our reading of the poem perceptibly. Browning did not read it as we read it now. The word "precursor" is indispensable in the vocabulary of criticism, but one should try to purify it from every connotation of polemic or rivalry. The fact is that each writer *creates* his precursors. His work modifies our conception of the past, as it will modify the future.[2] In this correlation the identity or plurality of men matters not at all. The first Kafka of *Betrachtung* is less a precursor of the Kafka of the shadowy myths and atrocious institutions than is Browning or Lord Dunsany.

Buenos Aires, 1951

[2] See T. S. Eliot, *Points of View* (1941), pp. 25–26.

Avatars of the Tortoise

One concept corrupts and confuses the others. I am not speaking of the Evil whose limited sphere is ethics; I am speaking of the infinite. Once I wanted to compile its changeable history. The abundant Hydra (the marshy monster that becomes a prefiguration or symbol of geometric progressions) would provide suitable horror for its beginning; Kafka's sordid nightmares would complete it; and its central chapters would not be unacquainted with the conjectures of that remote German Cardinal—Nicholas de Krebs, Nicholas de Cusa—who saw a polygon with an infinite number of angles in the circumference and wrote that an infinite line would be a straight line, would be a triangle, would be a circle and a sphere (*De docta ignorantia*, I, 13). Five, seven years of metaphysical, theological, and mathematical apprenticeship would (perhaps) enable me to plan that book properly. I need not add that life denies me that hope, and even that adverb.

These pages belong to that illusory *Biography of the Infinite*. Their purpose is to record certain avatars of Zeno's second Paradox.

Let us recall that Paradox now. Achilles runs ten times faster than the tortoise and gives him a start of ten meters. Achilles runs those ten meters, the tortoise runs one; Achilles runs that meter, the tortoise runs a decimeter; Achilles runs that decimeter, the tortoise

109

runs a centimeter; Achilles runs that centimeter, the tortoise, a milli-meter; Achilles the Nimble-Footed, the millimeter, the tortoise a tenth of a millimeter, and so on ad infinitum, with Achilles never overtaking the tortoise. This is the usual version. Wilhelm Capelle (*Die Vorsokratiker*, 1935, p. 178) translates Aristotle's original text as follows: "Zeno's second argument is the so-called Achilles argu-ment. He reasons that the slower will not be overtaken by the faster, because the pursuer has to pass through the place that the pursued has just vacated, so the slower always has a decided advantage." The problem does not change, as we see; but I should like to know the name of the poet who endowed it with a hero and a tortoise! The argument owes its diffusion to those magical competitors and to the series

$$10 + 1 + \frac{1}{10} + \frac{1}{100} + \frac{1}{1,000} + \frac{1}{10,000} + \cdots$$

Scarcely anyone remembers the argument that precedes it—the one about the racecourse—although its mechanism is identical. Movement is impossible (argues Zeno) because before a moving body can reach a given point, it must traverse half of the distance, and before that, half of the half, and before that, half of the half of the half, and before that—[1]

We are indebted to Aristotle for the divulgation and the first refutation of those arguments. He refutes them with a perhaps dis-dainful brevity, but the memory of them inspires his famous *argu-ment of the third man* against the Platonic doctrine, which seeks to demonstrate that two individuals who have common attributes (for example, two men) are mere temporal appearances of an eternal archetype. Aristotle asks if the many men and the Man—the tem-poral individuals and the Archetype—have common attributes. It is obvious that they do: they have the general attributes of humanity. In that case, states Aristotle, it will be necessary to postulate *another* archetype that includes them all, and then a fourth . . . In a note on his translation of the *Metaphysics*, Patricio de Azcárate attributes this presentation to one of Aristotle's disciples:

[1] A century later the Chinese sophist Hui Tzu reasoned that a stick cut in half each day would be interminable (H. A. Giles, *Chuang Tzu* [1889], p. 453).

110

If there is a separate being that incorporates the attributes of many different beings, and is different from them (as the Platonists claim), then there must be a third man. *Man* is a term applied to the individuals and to the idea as well. There is, then, a third man in addition to the individual men and the idea. At the same time, there is a fourth who will be in the same relation to the third and to the idea and to the individual men; then a fifth and so on ad infinitum.

Let us postulate two individuals, *a* and *b*, who make up class *c*. Then we shall have

$$a + b = c.$$

But also, according to Aristotle,

$$a + b + c = d$$
$$a + b + c + d = e$$
$$a + b + c + d + e = f \ldots$$

Two individuals are not actually needed; the individual and the class are enough to determine the third man postulated by Aristotle. Zeno of Elea uses infinite regression to deny movement and number; his refuter uses infinite regression to deny universal forms.[2]

The next avatar of Zeno I find in my disordered notes is Agrippa, the skeptic. He denies that anything can be proved, because every

[2] In the *Parmenides*—which is undeniably Zenonian in tone—Plato invents a very similar argument to show that the one is really many. If the one exists, it partakes of being; therefore, there are two parts in it, one and being; but each of these parts also has in turn both one and being, so that it is made up of two parts, and every part has these two parts, for the same principle goes on forever. Russell (*Introduction to Mathematical Philosophy* [1919], p. 138), substitutes an arithmetical progression for Plato's geometrical progression. If the one exists, the one partakes of being; but as one and being are different, two exist; but as being and two are different, three exist, etc. Chuang Tzu (Waley, *Three Ways of Thought in Ancient China*, p. 25) utilizes the same interminable *regressus* against the monists who declared that the Ten Thousand Things (the Universe) are one single thing. "Because," he argues, "cosmic unity and the declaration of that unity are already two things; those two and the declaration of their duality are already three; those three and the declaration of their trinity are already four." Russell is of the opinion that the vagueness of the term *being* is sufficient to invalidate the reasoning. He adds that numbers do not exist, that they are mere fictions of logic.

proof requires a previous proof (*Hypotyposes*, I, 166). Sextus Empyricus argues similarly that definitions are useless, because one would have to define each of the words used and then one would have to define the definition (*Hypotyposes*, II, 207). Sixteen hundred years later Byron will write of Coleridge in the dedication to *Don Juan*, "I wish he would explain his Explanation."

Thus far, the *regressus in infinitum* has been used in a negative way. St. Thomas Aquinas makes use of it (*Summa Theologica*, I, 2, 3) to affirm that God exists. He observes that all things in the universe have an efficient cause and that this cause, naturally, is the effect of a previous cause. The world is an interminable concatenation of causes and each cause is an effect. Each state proceeds from the previous one and determines the following one, but the general series could have *not* existed, since the terms that form it are conditional, that is, fortuitous. Nevertheless, the world *is*; from that fact we can infer a noncontingent first cause, which will be the divinity. This is the cosmological proof; Aristotle and Plato prefigure it; Leibnitz rediscovers it.[3]

Hermann Lotze uses the *regressus* as a way not to understand that an alteration of object *A* can produce an alteration of object *B*. He reasons that if *A* and *B* are independent, then to postulate an influence of *A* on *B* is to postulate a third element *C*, which to operate on *B* will require a fourth element *D*, which will not be able to operate without *E*, which will not be able to operate without *F* . . . To elude that multiplication of chimeras, he concludes that there is one single object in the world: an infinite and absolute substance, comparable to the God of Spinoza. The transferable causes are reduced to immanent ones; events, to manifestations or forms of the cosmic substance.[4]

Analogous, but even more alarming, is the case of F. H. Bradley. This thinker (*Appearance and Reality*, 1897, pp. 19–34) does not stop at combating the causal relationship; he denies all relationships.

[3] An echo of that proof, which is now dead, is heard in the first verse of the *Paradiso*: *La gloria di Colui che tutto move*.
[4] I am following the exposition of James (*A Pluralistic Universe* [1909], pp. 55–60). Cf. Wentscher, *Fechner und Lotze* (1924), pp. 166–171.

112

He asks if a relationship is related to its terms. The answer is yes, and he infers that this is to admit the existence of two other relationships, and then of two others. In the axiom "the part is smaller than the whole" he does not perceive two terms and the relationship "smaller than"; he perceives three (*part, smaller than, whole*); uniting them implies two other relationships, and so on to infinity. In the proposition "John is mortal" he perceives three unjoinable concepts (the third is the copula) which we shall never completely unite. He transforms all concepts into isolated, very solid subjects. To refute him is to contaminate one's self with unreality.

Lotze interposes Zeno's periodic abysses between the cause and the effect; Bradley, between the subject and the predicate, if not between the subject and the attributes; Lewis Carroll (*Mind*, Vol. IV, p. 278), between the second premise of the syllogism and the conclusion. He relates an endless dialogue between Achilles and the tortoise. When they have reached the end of their interminable race, the two athletes converse calmly about geometry. They study this clear syllogism:

a)   Two things equal to a third are equal to each other.
b)   The two sides of this triangle are equal to MN.
z)   The two sides of this triangle are equal to each other.

The tortoise accepts the premises a and b, but denies that they justify the conclusion. He induces Achilles to interpolate a hypothetical proposition.

a)   Two things equal to a third are equal to each other.
b)   The two sides of this triangle are equal to MN.
c)   If a and b are valid, z is valid.
z)   The two sides of this triangle are equal to each other.

After this brief clarification the tortoise accepts the validity of a, b, and c, but not of z. Indignantly Achilles interpolates:

d)   If a, b, and c are valid, z is valid.

And then, somewhat resignedly:

e)   If a, b, c, and d are valid, z is valid.

113

Carroll observes that the Greek's paradox allows an infinite series of diminishing distances, and that in the paradox he proposes the distances increase.

Here is a final example, perhaps the most elegant of all, but also the least different from Zeno. William James (*Some Problems of Philosophy*, 1911, p. 182) denies that fourteen minutes can elapse, because before they do, seven must have elapsed; and before seven, three and one-half minutes; and before three and one-half, a minute and three-fourths; and so on to the end, to the invisible end, through the tenuous labyrinths of time.

Descartes, Hobbes, Leibnitz, Mill, Renouvier, Georg Cantor, Gomperz, Russell, and Bergson have formulated explanations—not always inexplicable and vain—of the paradox of the tortoise. (I recorded several in *Discusión*, 1932, pp. 151–161.) Their applications are copious also, as the reader has been able to verify. Not only the historical ones: the vertiginous *regressus in infinitum* can perhaps be applied to all subjects. To aesthetics: a certain verse moves us for a certain reason, a certain reason for a certain other reason. To the problem of knowledge: to know is to recognize, but it is necessary to have known in order to recognize, but to know is to recognize. How can we judge this sort of dialectic? Is it a legitimate instrument of inquiry or merely a bad habit?

It is hazardous to think that a coordination of words (philosophies are nothing else) can have much resemblance to the universe. It is also hazardous to think that one of those famous coordinations does not resemble it a little more than others, even in an infinitesimal way. I have examined those that enjoy a certain prestige. I would even assert that the only one in which I recognize some vestige of the universe is that formulated by Schopenhauer. According to his doctrine, the world is a fabrication of the will. Art—always—requires visible unrealities. Let me cite but one example: the metaphorical or rhythmical or studiedly casual diction of the characters in a play. Let us admit what all idealists admit: that the nature of the world is hallucinatory. Let us do what no idealist has done: let us look for the unrealities that confirm that nature. We shall find them, I believe, in the antinomies of Kant and in Zeno's dialectic.

114

"The greatest sorcerer [writes Novalis memorably] would be the one who bewitched himself to the point of taking his own phantasmagorias for autonomous apparitions. Would not this be true of us?"

I believe that it is. We (the undivided divinity that operates within us) have dreamed the world. We have dreamed it strong, mysterious, visible, ubiquitous in space and secure in time; but we have allowed tenuous, eternal interstices of injustice in its structure so we may know that it is false.

1939

On the Cult of Books

In Book VIII of the *Odyssey* we read that the gods weave misfortunes into the pattern of events to make a song for future generations to sing. Mallarmé's statement that the world exists in order to be written in a book seems to repeat, some thirty centuries later, the same concept of an aesthetic justification for evils. The two teleologies, however, do not coincide fully; the Greek's belongs to the era of the spoken word, and the Frenchman's, to an era of the written word. One mentions song and the other mentions books. A book, any book, is a sacred object for us; Cervantes, who perhaps did not listen to everything people said, read even "the scraps of torn paper in the streets." In one of Bernard Shaw's plays, the library at Alexandria is threatened by fire; someone exclaims that the memory of mankind will burn, and Caesar says: "A shameful memory. Let it burn." In my opinion the historical Caesar would approve or condemn the command that the author attributes to him, but he would not consider it, as we do, a sacrilegious joke. The reason is clear: for the ancients the written word was merely a succedaneum of the spoken word.

It is said that Pythagoras did not write. Gomperz (*Griechische Denker*, 1, 3) maintains that it was because he had more faith in the virtues of spoken instruction. More forceful than the mere abstention of Pythagoras is Plato's unequivocal testimony. In the *Timaeus* he

116

stated: "It is an arduous task to discover the maker and father of this universe, and, after discovering him, it is impossible to declare him to all men." In the *Phaedrus* he related an Egyptian fable against writing (the practice of which causes people to neglect the exercise of memory and to depend on symbols), and he said that books are like the painted figures "that seem to be alive, but do not answer a word to the questions they are asked." To attenuate or eliminate that difficulty, he conceived the philosophical dialogue. The teacher selects the pupil, but the book does not select its readers, who may be wicked or stupid. That Platonic scruple persists in the words of Clement of Alexandria, a man of pagan culture: "The most prudent course is not to write but to learn and teach by word of mouth, because what is written remains" (*Stromateis*), and in this other excerpt from the same treatise: "To write all things in a book is to leave a sword in the hands of a child," which also derives from the evangelical words: "Give not that which is holy unto the dogs, neither cast ye your pearls before swine, lest they trample them under their feet, and turn again and rend you" (St. Matthew 7:6). Those words were spoken by Jesus, the greatest of oral teachers, who once wrote some words on the ground, and no man read what He had written (St. John 8:6).

Clement of Alexandria wrote about his distrust of writing at the end of the second century. At the end of the fourth century the mental process began that would culminate, after many centuries, in the predominance of the written word over the spoken one, of the pen over the voice. An admirable stroke of fortune decreed that a writer was to establish the instant (and I am not exaggerating) when the vast process began. In Book Six of the *Confessions*, St. Augustine wrote:

When Ambrose read, his eyes moved over the pages, and his soul penetrated the meaning, without his uttering a word or moving his tongue. Many times—for no one was forbidden to enter, or announced to him —we saw him reading silently and never otherwise, and after a while we would go away, conjecturing that during the brief interval he used to refresh his spirit, free from the tumult of the business of others, he did not wish to be disturbed, for perhaps he feared that someone who was listening, hearing a difficult part of the text, might ask him to explain an

117

obscure passage or might wish to discuss it with him, and would thus prevent him from reading as many volumes as he desired. I believe that he read that way to preserve his voice, which was easily strained. In any case, whatever the man's purpose was, it was surely a good one.

St. Augustine was a disciple of St. Ambrose, Bishop of Milan, around the year 384. Thirteen years later in Numidia he wrote his *Confessions* and that singular spectacle still troubled him: a man in a room, with a book, reading without articulating the words.[1]

That man progressed directly from the written symbol to intuitive perception, omitting the mark of sonority; the strange art he initiated, the art of silent reading, was to lead to marvelous consequences. It would lead, many years later, to the concept of the book as an end in itself, not as a means to an end. (This mystical concept, transferred to profane literature, would produce the singular destinies of Flaubert and Mallarmé, of Henry James and James Joyce.) Superimposed on the notion of a God who speaks with men to order them to do something or to forbid them to do something is the notion of the Absolute Book, the notion of a Sacred Scripture. For the Moslems the Alcorán (also called The Book, *Al Kitab*) is not merely a work of God, like men's souls or the universe; it is one of the attributes of God like His eternity or His ire. In Chapter XIII we read that the original text, *The Mother of the Book*, is deposited in Heaven. Muhammad-al-Ghazali, the Algazel of the scholastics, declared: "The Koran is copied in a book, is pronounced with the tongue, is remembered in the heart and, even so, continues to persist in the center of God and is not altered by its passage through written pages and human understanding." George Sale observes that this increate Koran is nothing but its idea or Platonic archetype. Al-Ghazali may have utilized the archetypes that were communicated to Islam by the encyclopedia of the Brethren of Purity and by Avicenna to justify the notion of the Mother of the Book.

[1] Commentators have observed that it was customary at that time to read out loud in order to grasp the meaning better, for there were no punctuation marks, nor was there even a division of words; and to read in common because there was a scarcity of manuscripts. The dialogue of Lucian of Samosata, *Against an Ignorant Buyer of Books*, includes a testimony of that custom in the second century.

Even more extravagant than the Moslems were the Jews. The first chapter of the Jewish Bible contains the famous sentence: "And God said, Let there be light: and there was light." The cabalists reasoned that the virtue of that command from the Lord proceeded from the letters of the words. The *Sepher Yetzirah* (Book of the Formation), written in Syria or Palestine around the sixth century, reveals that Jehovah of the Armies, God of Israel, and God Omnipotent created the universe by means of the cardinal numbers that go from one to ten and the twenty-two letters of the alphabet. That numbers may be instruments or elements of the Creation is the dogma of Pythagoras and Iamblichus; that letters also may be used in the Creation is a clear indication of the new cult of writing. The second paragraph of the second chapter reads: "Twenty-two fundamental letters: God drew them, engraved them, combined them, weighed them, permuted them, and with them produced everything that is and everything that will be." Then the book reveals which letter has power over the air, which over water, which over fire, which over wisdom, which over peace, which over grace, which over sleep, which over anger, and how (for example) the letter *kaf*, which has power over life, was used to form the sun in the world, the day Wednesday in the year, and the left ear on the body.

The Christians went even further. The thought that the divinity had written a book moved them to imagine that he had written two, and that the other one was the universe. At the beginning of the seventeenth century Francis Bacon declared in his *Advancement of Learning* that God offered us two books so that we would not fall into error. The first, the volume of the Scriptures, reveals His will; the second, the volume of the creatures, reveals His power and is the key to the former. Bacon intended much more than the making of a metaphor; he believed that the world was reducible to essential forms (temperatures, densities, weights, colors), which integrated, in a limited number, an *abecedarium naturae* or series of the letters with which the universal text is written.[2] Around 1642 Sir Thomas Browne confirmed

[2] The concept of the universe as a book is prevalent in Galileo's works. The second section of Favaro's anthology (*Galileo Galilei: Pensieri, motti e sentenze* [Florence, 1949]) is entitled *Il libro della Natura*. I quote the following paragraph: "Philosophy is written in that very large book that is continually

119

that: "Thus there are two Books from whence I collect my Divinity; besides that written one of God, another of His servant Nature, that universal and publick Manuscript, that lies expans'd unto the Eyes of all: those that never saw Him in the one, have discover'd Him in the other" (*Religio Medici*, I, 16). In the same paragraph we read: "In brief, all things are artificial; for Nature is the Art of God."

Two hundred years passed, and the Scot Carlyle, in various of his works and particularly in the essay on Cagliostro, surpassed Bacon's conjecture; he said that universal history was a Sacred Scripture: one that we decipher and write uncertainly, and in which we also are written. Later, Léon Bloy would write:

There is no human being on earth who is capable of declaring who he is. No one knows what he has come to this world to do, to what his acts, feelings, ideas correspond, or what his real *name* is, his imperishable Name in the registry of Light . . . History is an immense liturgical text, where the *i*'s and the periods are not worth less than the versicles or whole chapters, but the importance of both is undeterminable and is profoundly hidden. (*L'Ame de Napoléon*, 1912)

According to Mallarmé, the world exists for a book; according to Bloy, we are the versicles or words or letters of a magic book, and that incessant book is the only thing in the world: or, rather, it is the world.

Buenos Aires, 1951

---

opened before our eyes (I mean the universe), but which is not understood unless first one studies the language and knows the characters in which it is written. The language of that book is mathematical and the characters are triangles, circles, and other geometric figures."

The Nightingale of Keats

Those who have frequented the lyric poetry of England will not forget the "Ode to a Nightingale" that John Keats, consumptive, poor, and perhaps unfortunate in love, composed in a Hampstead garden one April night in 1819 when he was twenty-three. In the garden Keats heard the eternal nightingale of Ovid and Shakespeare and felt his own mortality, contrasting it with the delicate imperishable voice of the invisible bird. Keats had written that the poet must give poetry naturally, as the tree gives leaves; two or three hours were all he needed to produce that page of inexhaustible and insatiable beauty, which he scarcely had to touch afterward. As far as I know, its virtue has never been questioned, but its interpretation has. The crux of the problem is found in the penultimate stanza. The circumstantial and mortal man addresses the bird, "No hungry generations tread thee down," whose voice, now, is the same heard by Ruth the Moabite on the fields of Israel one ancient afternoon.

In his monograph on Keats, published in 1887, Sidney Colvin (a correspondent and friend of Stevenson) perceived or invented a difficulty in the stanza I am speaking of. He made a curious statement that with an error of logic (which in his opinion was also a poetic fault) Keats opposed to the fugacity of human life, by which he meant the life of the individual, the permanence of the bird's life, by which

121

he meant the life of the species. In 1895 Bridges repeated the accusation; F. R. Leavis approved it in 1936 and added that the fallacy included in the concept naturally proved the intensity of the feeling that engendered it. In the first stanza of his poem Keats had called the nightingale a Dryad; another critic, Garrod, quoted that epithet in all seriousness to express the opinion that the bird was immortal because it was a dryad, a divinity of the forests. Amy Lowell wrote more accurately that the reader who had a spark of imaginative or poetic sense would perceive at once that Keats did not refer to the nightingale singing at that moment, but to the species.

Those are five opinions from five critics of the past and the present; of them all I find the dictum of the North American writer Amy Lowell the least vain; but I deny the opposition she postulated between the ephemeral nightingale of that night and the generic nightingale. I suspect that the key, the exact key to the stanza, is to be found in a metaphysical paragraph by Schopenhauer, who never read the poem.

The "Ode to a Nightingale" was written in 1819; the second volume of *The World as Will and Idea* appeared in 1844. In Chapter 41 we read:

Let us ask ourselves sincerely whether the swallow of this summer is a different one than the swallow of the first summer, and whether the miracle of bringing something forth from nothingness has really occurred millions of times between the two, to be mocked an equal number of times by absolute annihilation. Whoever hears me say that this cat playing here now is the same one that frolicked and romped in this place three hundred years ago may think of me what he will, but it is a stranger madness to imagine that he is fundamentally different.

In other words, the individual is somehow the species, and the nightingale of Keats is also the nightingale of Ruth.

Keats, who could write without exaggerated injustice that he knew nothing, that he had read nothing, divined the Greek spirit from the pages of a schoolboy's dictionary; a very subtle proof of that divination or re-creation is his intuitive recognition of the Platonic nightingale in the dark nightingale of a spring evening. Keats, who was perhaps incapable of defining the word *archetype*, anticipated one of Schopenhauer's theses by a quarter of a century.

122

Now that one difficulty has been clarified, there is still another one, of a very different nature. Why did Garrod and Leavis and the others not find this obvious interpretation?[1] Leavis was a professor at one of the colleges of Cambridge, the city that in the seventeenth century was the meeting place of the Cambridge Platonists and gave them their name; Bridges wrote a Platonic poem entitled "The Fourth Dimension"; the mere enumeration of those facts seems to aggravate the enigma. If I am not mistaken, the reason derives from something essential in the British mind.

Coleridge observes that all men are born Aristotelians or Platonists. The latter feel that classes, orders, and genres are realities; the former, that they are generalizations. For the latter, language is nothing but an approximative set of symbols; for the former, it is the map of the universe. The Platonist knows that the universe is somehow a cosmos, an order; that order, for the Aristotelian, can be an error or a fiction of our partial knowledge. Across the latitudes and the epochs, the two immortal antagonists change their name and language: one is Parmenides, Plato, Spinoza, Kant, Francis Bradley; the other, Heraclitus, Aristotle, Locke, Hume, William James. In the arduous schools of the Middle Ages they all invoke Aristotle, the master of human reason (*Convivio*, IV, 2), but the nominalists are Aristotle; the realists, Plato. The English nominalism of the fourteenth century reappears in the scrupulous English idealism of the eighteenth century; the economy of Occam's formula, *entia non sunt multiplicanda praeter necessitatem*, permits or prefigures the no less precise *esse est percipi*. Men, said Coleridge, are born Aristotelians or Platonists; one can state of the English mind that it was born Aristotelian. For that mind, not abstract concepts but individual ones are real; not the generic nightingale, but concrete nightingales. It is natural, it is perhaps inevitable, that in England the "Ode to a Nightingale" is not understood correctly.

Please do not read reprobation or disdain into the foregoing words. The Englishman rejects the generic because he feels that the indi-

[1] To these must be added the poet of genius, William Butler Yeats, who in the first stanza of "Sailing to Byzantium" speaks of "Those dying generations" of birds, with a deliberate or involuntary allusion to the "Ode." See T. R. Henn, *The Lonely Tower* (1950), p. 211.

vidual is irreducible, unassimilable, and unique. An ethical scruple, not a speculative incapacity, prevents him from trafficking in abstractions like the German. He does not understand the "Ode to a Nightingale"; that estimable incomprehension permits him to be Locke, to be Berkeley, to be Hume, and to write (around seventy years ago) the unheeded and prophetic admonitions about the individual against the State.

In all the languages of the world the nightingale enjoys a melodious name (*ruiseñor, nachtigall, usignolo,* for example), as if men instinctively wished the name to be not unworthy of the song that filled them with wonder. Poets have exalted it to such an extent that it has come to be a little unreal, less akin to the lark than to the angel. From the Saxon enigmas of *The Exeter Book,* where it is called the ancient singer of the evening that brings joy to the noblemen, to Swinburne's tragic *Atalanta,* the infinite nightingale has sung in English literature. Chaucer and Shakespeare extol it, and Milton and Matthew Arnold, but we inevitably attach its image to John Keats, as we attach the tiger's to Blake.

The Mirror of the Enigmas

The notion that the Sacred Scripture possesses (in addition to its literal meaning) a symbolic one is not irrational and is ancient: it is found in Philo of Alexandria, in the cabalists, in Swedenborg. Since the events related by the Scripture are true (God is Truth, the Truth cannot lie, et cetera), we must admit that as men acted out those events they were blindly performing a secret drama determined and premeditated by God. There is not an infinite distance from this thought to the idea that the history of the universe—and our lives and the most trifling detail of our lives—has an unconjecturable, symbolic meaning. Many people must have traveled this distance, but no one so astonishingly as Léon Bloy. In the psychological fragments by Novalis and in the volume of Machen's autobiography entitled *The London Adventure* may be found a similar hypothesis: the external world—forms, temperatures, the moon—is a language that we humans have forgotten, or one that we can scarcely decipher. De Quincey made the same declaration: "Even the articulate or brutal sounds of the globe must be all so many languages and ciphers that somewhere have their corresponding keys—have their own grammar and syntax; and thus the least things in the universe must be secret mirrors to the greatest" (*Autobiography*, Chap. IV).

A versicle from St. Paul (I Corinthians 13:12) inspired Léon

Bloy. "Videmus nunc per speculum in aenigmate: tunc autem facie ad faciem. Nunc cognosco ex parte: tunc autem cognoscam sicut et cognitus sum." And in Torres Amat's wretched translation: "Al presente no vemos *a Dios* sino como en un espejo, y bajo imágenes oscuras: pero entonces *le* veremos cara a cara. Yo no *le* conozco ahora sino imperfectamente: mas entonces *le* conoceré *con una visión clara,* a la manera que soy yo conocido." ("At present we see *God* only as in a mirror, and under obscure semblances: but then we shall see *Him* face to face. I know *Him* only imperfectly now: but then I shall know *Him with a clear vision,* as I myself am known.") Forty-four words do the work of twenty-two; it is impossible to be more wordy and more languid. Cipriano de Valera is more faithful to the original: "Now we see through a mirror, in darkness; but then *we shall see* face to face. Now I know in part; but then I shall know as I am known." Torres Amat opines that the versicle refers to our vision of the divinity; Cipriano de Valera (and Léon Bloy), to our general vision.

As far as I know, Bloy did not put his conjecture into definitive form. All through his fragmentary work (which, as no one is unaware, abounds in lamentation and invective) different versions or facets of it appear. Here are several of them, which I have salvaged from the clamorous pages of *Le mendiant ingrat, Le Vieux de la Montagne,* and *L'invendable.* I do not believe that I have found them all: I hope that an authority on Léon Bloy (I am not one) will complete and amend my examples.

The first is from June, 1894. I translate it as follows:

The sentence from St. Paul, *Videmus nunc per speculum in aenigmate,* would be a skylight for plunging into the true Abyss, which is man's soul. The terrifying immensity of the abyss of the firmament is an illusion, an outward reflection of *our* abysses, perceived "in a mirror." We must invert our eyes and practice a sublime astronomy in the infinity of our hearts, the hearts God died for . . . If we see the Milky Way, that is because it *truly* exists in our soul.

The second is from November of the same year:

I remember one of my earliest ideas. The Czar is the leader and spiritual father of one hundred and fifty million men. An atrocious responsibility, which is merely an apparent one. Perhaps he is not responsible, before God, for more than a few human beings. If the poor people of his empire are oppressed during his reign, if immense catastrophes result from that reign, who knows whether the servant in charge of polishing his boots is not the real and only culprit? In the mysterious dispositions of the Profundity, who is really a Czar, who is a king, who can boast of being a mere servant?

The third is from a letter written in December:

Everything is a symbol, even the most tortuous pain. We are sleepers who shout in our sleep. We do not know if the thing that afflicts us is the secret beginning of our future joy. We see now, St. Paul says, *per speculum in aenigmate*, literally: "in enigma by means of a mirror" and we shall not see otherwise until the advent of The One Who is all in flames and who must reveal all things to us.

The fourth is from May, 1904: *"Per speculum in aenigmate*, says St. Paul. We see everything in reverse. When we think we are giving, we receive, etc. Then (a dear anguished soul tells me) we are in heaven and God suffers on earth."

The fifth is from May, 1908: "A terrifying idea, that of Jeanne, about the text *per speculum*. The joys of this world would be the torments of hell, seen *in reverse*, in a mirror."

The sixth is from 1912. It is each one of the pages of *L'Ame de Napoléon*, a book whose purpose is to decipher the symbol *Napoléon*, considered as the precursor of another hero—a man and a symbol— who is hidden in the future. I shall quote only two passages: "Each man is on earth to symbolize something he does not know and to realize a particle, or a mountain, of the invisible material that will serve to build the City of God."

There is no human being on earth who is capable of declaring who he is, with certainty. No one knows what he has come to this world to do, to what his acts, feelings, ideas correspond, or what his real *name* is, his imperishable Name in the registry of Light . . . History is an immense liturgical text, where the *i*'s and the periods are not worth less than whole verses or chapters, but the importance of both is undeterminable and is profoundly hidden.

The foregoing paragraphs may seem to the reader like mere gratuities from Bloy. As far as I know, he never thought of trying to justify them with reason. I venture to consider them plausible, and perhaps inevitable within the Christian doctrine. Bloy (I repeat) did nothing but apply to the whole Creation the method that the Jewish cabalists applied to the Scripture. They thought that a work dictated by the Holy Spirit was an absolute text: a text where the collaboration of chance is calculable at zero. The portentous premise of a book that is impervious to contingency, a book that is a mechanism of infinite purposes, moved them to permute the scriptural words, to sum up the numerical value of the letters, to consider their form, to observe the small letters and the capital letters, to search for acrostics and anagrams; and it led them to other easily ridiculed exegetic rigors. The apology of such a premise is that nothing can be contingent in the work of an infinite intelligence.[1] Léon Bloy postulates that hieroglyphical quality—the quality of divine writing, of a cryptography of the angels—in all the instants and in all the beings of the world. The superstitious man believes he penetrates that organic writing: thirteen commensals articulate the symbol of death; a yellow opal, the symbol of misfortune.

It is doubtful that the world has a meaning; it is more doubtful still, the incredulous will observe, that it has a double and triple meaning. I agree; but I believe that the hieroglyphic world postulated by Bloy best befits the dignity of the intellectual God of the theologians.

"No one knows who he is," said Léon Bloy. Who could have illustrated that intimate ignorance better than he? He believed himself to be a strict Catholic and he was a continuer of the cabalists, a secret brother of Swedenborg and Blake: heresiarchs.

---

[1] What is an infinite intelligence? the reader may ask. All theologians define it; I prefer to give an example. The steps a man takes, from the day of his birth to the day of his death, trace an inconceivable figure in time. The Divine Intelligence perceives that figure at once, as man's intelligence perceives a triangle. That figure (perhaps) has its determined function in the economy of the universe.

Two Books

Wells's last book—*Guide to the New World: A Handbook of Constructive World Revolution*—may seem, at first glance, like a mere encyclopedia of vituperation. His very legible pages denounce the Fuehrer, who squeals "like a gripped rabbit"; Goering, who " 'destroys' towns overnight and they resume work and sweep up their broken glass in the morning"; Eden, who, "having wedded himself to the poor dead League of Nations, still cannot believe it dead"; Joseph Stalin, who in an unreal jargon continues to vindicate the dictatorship of the proletariat, although "nobody knows really what and where this 'proletariat' is, still less do they know how and where it dictates"; "the absurd Ironside"; the generals of the French army, "beaten by a sudden realisation of their own unpreparedness and incompetence, by tanks that had been made in Czechoslovakia, by radio voices around them and behind them, messenger boys on motor bicycles who told them to surrender"; the "positive will for defeat in high quarters"; the "spite slum, Southern Ireland"; the British Foreign Office and diplomatic service, which, although "the Germans have already lost it [the war], seem to be doing their utmost to throw it back to them"; Sir Samuel Hoare, "this *silly* man—there really is no other word for him; he is not only silly mentally but morally silly";

the Americans and English who betrayed the liberal cause in Spain; those who believe the war is a war of ideologies and not a criminal formula of the current disorder; the ingenuous souls who believe that merely to exorcise or destroy the demons Goering and Hitler will make the world a paradise.

I have assembled some of Wells's invective, which is not memorable from a literary standpoint and is, in some cases, unjust; but it reveals the impartiality of his hatred or his indignation. It also reveals the freedom enjoyed by writers in England during wartime. More important than his epigrammatic dudgeon (the few examples I have given could easily be tripled or quadrupled) is the doctrine of this revolutionary manual, which can be summarized in this precise dilemma: either Britain identifies her cause with that of a general revolution (with that of a federated world), or victory is inaccessible and vain. Chapter XII (pp. 48–54) establishes the basic principles of the new world. The three final chapters discuss some lesser problems.

Wells, incredibly, is not a Nazi. I say incredibly, because nearly all my contemporaries are, although they either deny it or are not aware of it. Since 1925 no writer has failed to maintain that the inevitable and trivial circumstance of having been born in a certain country and of belonging to a certain race (or mixture of races) is a singular privilege and an effective talisman. Those who vindicate democracy, who believe themselves to be very different from Goebbels, urge their readers, in the enemy's own words, to heed the beating of a heart that answers the call of the blood and the land.

I recall certain rather undecipherable discussions that took place during the Spanish Civil War. Some people declared that they were Republicans; others, Nationalists; still others, Marxists; yet they all, in a Gauleiter lexicon, spoke of the Race and the People. Even the men of the hammer and sickle turned out to be racists. I also recall with some amazement a certain assembly that was convoked to condemn anti-Semitism. For several reasons I am not anti-Semitic; the principal one is that I generally find the difference between Jews and non-Jews quite insignificant, and sometimes illusory or imperceptible. But on that particular day no one wished to share my opinion; they all swore that a German Jew was vastly different from a German. In vain I reminded them that Adolf Hitler said the same thing; in vain

130

I insinuated that an assembly against racism should not tolerate the doctrine of a Superior Race; in vain I quoted the wise declaration of Mark Twain that a man's race was unimportant, for, after all, he was a human being, and no one could be anything worse.

In this book, as in others—*The Fate of Homo Sapiens* (1939), *The Common Sense of War and Peace* (1940)—Wells admonishes us to remember our essential humanity and to suppress our miserable differential traits, no matter how pathetic or picturesque they may be. Such suppression is in no way exorbitant; it merely demands of states, for their peaceful coexistence, what an elementary courtesy demands of individuals. Wells states that no one in his right mind views the British as members of a superior race, a more noble species of Nazis, who are disputing the hegemony of the world with the Germans, but affirms that they are the battle front of humanity; and, if they are not that, they are nothing. And, he adds, that duty is a privilege.

Let the People Think is the title of a selection of essays by Bertrand Russell. In the work by Wells I outlined above, we are urged to reconsider the history of the world without geographical, economic, or ethnic preferences; Russell also gives advice of a universal nature. In the third article, "Free Thought and Official Propaganda," he suggests that elementary schools should teach the art of reading newspapers with incredulity. That Socratic discipline would be useful, I believe. Very few of the persons I know have any acquaintance with it. They let themselves be deceived by typographical or syntactical tricks. They think that an event has occurred because it is printed in large black letters. They do not wish to understand that the statement "All the aggressor's attempts to advance beyond B have failed miserably" is merely a euphemistic way to admit the loss of B. What is even worse, they practice a kind of magic: they believe that to express any fear is to collaborate with the enemy. Russell proposes that the State endeavor to immunize its citizens against such deception and trickery. For example, he suggests that school children should study the *Moniteur* bulletins, which were ostensibly triumphant, to learn about Napoléon's last defeats. A typical assignment would be to read about the history of the wars with France in English textbooks, and then to rewrite that history from the French viewpoint. Here in Argentina our "nationalists" have already adopted that paradoxical method: they

131

teach Argentine history from a Spanish, and even Quechua or Querendí, viewpoint.

Not the least apropos of the other articles is the one entitled "Genealogy of Fascism." The author begins by observing that political events issue from earlier speculations, and that much time may elapse between the divulging of a doctrine and its application. And so it is: the burning reality, which exasperates or exalts us and frequently annihilates us, is nothing but an imperfect reverberation of former discussions. Hitler, dreadful with his public armies and secret spies, is a pleonasm of Carlyle (1795–1881) and even of J. G. Fichte (1762–1814); Lenin, a transcription of Karl Marx. That is why the true intellectual eschews contemporary debates; reality is always anachronous.

Russell imputes the theory of fascism to Fichte and Carlyle. In the fourth and fifth of the famous *Reden an die deutsche Nation*, Fichte attributes the superiority of the Germans to their uninterrupted possession of a pure language. This statement is almost inexhaustibly fallacious. We can conjecture that there is no pure language on this earth (even if the words were, the representations are not; although purists say *deporte*, they write *sport*); we can recall that German is less "pure" than Basque or Hottentot; we can ask why an unmixed language should be preferable to a mixed one.

Carlyle's contribution is more complex and more eloquent. In 1843 he wrote that democracy was the despair of not finding heroes to lead us. In 1870 he acclaimed the victory of patient, noble, profound, solid, and pious Germany over boastful, proud, gesticulatory, quarrelsome, restless, hypersensitive France (*Miscellanies*, Vol. VII). He praised the Middle Ages, condemned the windbags of Parliament, vindicated the memory of the god Thor, of William the Bastard, Knox, Cromwell, Frederick II, the taciturn Dr. Francia, and Napoléon. He yearned for a world that was not chaos equipped with ballot boxes; he deplored the abolition of slavery; he proposed that statues, horrible bronze solecisms, be converted into useful bronze bathtubs; he praised the death penalty; he rejoiced that every town had a barracks; he flattered, and invented, the Teutonic Race. Those who wish for other imprecations or apotheoses can consult *Past and Present* (1843) and the *Latter-Day Pamphlets* (1850).

132

Bertrand Russell concludes that it is somehow licit to affirm that the atmosphere at the beginning of the eighteenth century was rational, and that the atmosphere of our time is antirational. I would omit the timid adverb *somehow*.

A Comment on August 23, 1944

That crowded day gave me three heterogeneous surprises: the *physical* happiness I experienced when they told me that Paris had been liberated; the discovery that a collective emotion can be noble; the enigmatic and obvious enthusiasm of many who were supporters of Hitler. I know that if I question that enthusiasm I may easily resemble those futile hydrographers who asked why a single ruby was enough to arrest the course of a river; many will accuse me of trying to explain a chimerical occurrence. Still, that was what happened and thousands of persons in Buenos Aires can bear witness to it.

From the beginning, I knew that it was useless to ask the people themselves. They are changeable; through their practice of incoherence they have lost every notion that incoherence should be justified: they venerate the German race, but they abhor "Saxon" America; they condemn the articles of Versailles, but they applaud the marvels of the Blitzkrieg; they are anti-Semitic, but they profess a religion of Hebrew origin; they laud submarine warfare, but they vigorously condemn acts of piracy by the British; they denounce imperialism, but they vindicate and promulgate the theory of *Lebensraum*; they idolize San Martín, but they regard the independence of America as a mistake; they apply the canon of Jesus to the acts of England, but the canon of Zarathustra to those of Germany.

134

I also reflected that every other uncertainty was preferable to the uncertainty of a dialogue with those siblings of chaos, who are exonerated from honor and piety by the infinite repetition of the interesting formula *I am Argentine*. And further, did Freud not reason and Walt Whitman not foresee that men have very little knowledge about the real motives for their conduct? Perhaps, I said to myself, the magic of the symbols *Paris* and *liberation* is so powerful that Hitler's partisans have forgotten that these symbols mean a defeat of his forces. Wearily, I chose to imagine that fickleness and fear and simple adherence to reality were the probable explanations of the problem.

Several nights later a book and a memory enlightened me. The book was Shaw's *Man and Superman*; the passage in question is the one about John Tanner's metaphysical dream, where it is stated that the horror of Hell is its unreality. That doctrine can be compared with the doctrine of another Irishman, Johannes Scotus Erigena, who denied the substantive existence of sin and evil and declared that all creatures, including the Devil, will return to God. The memory was of the day that is the exact and detested opposite of August 23, 1944: June 14, 1940. A certain Germanophile, whose name I do not wish to remember, came to my house that day. Standing in the doorway, he announced the dreadful news: the Nazi armies had occupied Paris. I felt a mixture of sadness, disgust, malaise. And then it occurred to me that his insolent joy did not explain the stentorian voice or the abrupt proclamation. He added that the German troops would soon be in London. Any opposition was useless, nothing could prevent their victory. That was when I knew that he too was terrified.

I do not know whether the facts I have related require elucidation. I believe I can interpret them like this: for Europeans and Americans, one order—and only one—is possible: it used to be called Rome and now it is called Western Culture. To be a Nazi (to play the game of energetic barbarism, to play at being a Viking, a Tartar, a sixteenth-century conquistador, a Gaucho, a redskin) is, after all, a mental and moral impossibility. Nazism suffers from unreality, like Erigena's hells. It is uninhabitable; men can only die for it, lie for it, kill and wound for it. No one, in the intimate depths of his being, can wish it to triumph. I shall hazard this conjecture: *Hitler wants to be defeated.*

135

Hitler is collaborating blindly with the inevitable armies that will annihilate him, as the metal vultures and the dragon (which must not have been unaware that they were monsters) collaborated, mysteriously, with Hercules.

About William Beckford's *Vathek*

Wilde attributes the following joke to Carlyle: a biography of Michelangelo that would omit any mention of Michelangelo's works. Reality is so complex, history is so fragmentary and so simplified, that an omniscient observer could write an indefinite, and almost infinite, number of biographies of a man, each of which would emphasize different facts; we would have to read many of them before we realized that the protagonist was the same man. Simplify a life overmuch: imagine that thirteen thousand facts describe it completely. One of the hypothetical biographies would record the series 11, 22, 33 . . . ; another, the series 9, 13, 17, 21 . . . ; another, the series 3, 12, 21, 30, 39 . . . A history of a man's dreams is not inconceivable; or of the organs of his body; or of the mistakes he has made; or of all the moments when he imagined the Pyramids; or of his traffic with night and with dawn. What I have just written may seem to be mere fancy, but alas! it is not. No one resigns himself to writing the literary biography of an author, the military biography of a soldier. Everyone prefers the genealogical biography, the economic biography, the psychiatric biography, the surgical biography, the topographical biography. One life of Poe consists of seven hundred octavo pages. The biographer, fascinated by Poe's changes of residence, barely manages to salvage one parenthesis for the "Maelstrom" and

137

the cosmogony of "Eureka." Another example: this curious revelation in the prologue to a biography of Bolívar—that the book contained as little mention of battles as did the same author's previous work about Napoléon. Carlyle's joke was a prefiguring of our contemporary literature: a biography of Michelangelo that permits some mention of his works is the paradox now!

My perusal of a recent biography of William Beckford (1760–1844) has inspired the foregoing observations. William Beckford of Fonthill was a rather ordinary sort of millionaire—a distinguished gentleman, a traveler, a bibliophile, a builder of palaces, and a libertine. Chapman, his biographer, fathoms (or tries to fathom) his labyrinthine life, but omits an analysis of the novel *Vathek*, on the final ten pages of which Beckford's fame rests.

I have compared several different criticisms of *Vathek*. The prologue Mallarmé wrote for the 1876 edition contains a wealth of happy pronouncements (for example, he points out that the novel begins atop a tower from which the secrets of heaven are penetrated, and ends in an enchanted subterranean vault), but he wrote it in an etymological dialect of French that is difficult or impossible to read. Belloc (*A Conversation with an Angel*, 1928), without condescending to reasons, compares Beckford's prose to Voltaire's and judges him to be "one of the vilest men of his time." Perhaps the most lucid evaluation of Beckford is Saintsbury's in the eleventh volume of the *Cambridge History of English Literature*.

Essentially the fable of *Vathek* is not complex. Vathek (Haroun Benalmotasim Vatiq Bilá, the ninth Abbasid caliph) builds a Babylonian tower in order to decipher the planets, which foretell a succession of wonders to be brought about by a strange-looking man who will come from an unknown land. A merchant arrives at the capital of the empire; his face is so atrocious that the guards who lead him into the presence of the caliph advance with closed eyes. The merchant sells a scimitar to the caliph and then disappears. Carved on the blade are some mysterious changing characters which pique Vathek's curiosity. A man (who soon disappears also) deciphers them. One day they mean: "I am the least of the marvels in a place where everything is marvelous and worthy of the greatest Prince of the earth"; another day they mean: "Woe to the rash mortal who

138

aspires to know that which he is not supposed to know." The caliph surrenders to the art of magic. From the shadows the merchant's voice urges him to abjure the Moslem faith and adore the powers of darkness. If he will do that, the Palace of Subterranean Fire will be opened to him. Within its vaults he will be able to contemplate the treasures that the stars have promised, the talismans that subdue the world, the diadems of the pre-Adamite sultans and of Suleiman Ben Daoud. The greedy caliph agrees; the merchant demands fifty human sacrifices. Many bloody years pass. Vathek, his soul black with abomination, arrives at a deserted mountain. The earth opens; terrified and hopeful, Vathek descends to the bottom of the world. A silent, pale crowd of persons who do not look at one another wanders through the superb galleries of an infinite palace. The merchant did not lie: the Palace of Subterranean Fire abounds in splendors and talismans, but it is also Hell. (In the congenerous story of Doctor Faustus and the many medieval legends that prefigured it, Hell is the punishment of the sinner who makes a pact with the gods of Evil; in this story, Hell is the punishment and the temptation.)

Saintsbury and Andrew Lang declare or suggest that the invention of the Palace of Subterranean Fire is Beckford's greatest achievement. I maintain that it is the first truly atrocious Hell in literature.[1] And I shall hazard this paradox: the most famous literary Avernus, the *dolente regno* of the *Divine Comedy*, is not an atrocious place; it is a place where atrocious things happen. The distinction is valid.

Stevenson ("A Chapter on Dreams") tells of being haunted in the dreams of his childhood by nothing more definite than a certain hue of brown; Chesterton (*The Man Who Was Thursday*, VI) imagines that at the western boundary of the world there may be a tree which is already more, or less, than a tree; and that at the opposite end of the world, something, a tower, the very shape of which is wicked. Poe, in his "MS Found in a Bottle," speaks of a sea where the ship grows in volume like the living body of the seaman; Melville devotes many pages of *Moby Dick* to an elucidation of the insupportable whiteness of the whale.

---

[1] In literature, I repeat, not in mystic lore: the elective Hell of Swedenborg —*De coelo et inferno*, 545, 554—is of an earlier date.

I have given several examples; perhaps the observation that Dante's Hell magnifies the notion of a jail, and Beckford's, the tunnels of a nightmare, would have sufficed. The *Divine Comedy* is the most justifiable and the most solid work in all literature, *Vathek* is a mere curiosity, "the perfume and suppliance of a minute"; and yet I believe that *Vathek* prognosticates, at least in a rudimentary way, the satanic splendors of Thomas de Quincey and Poe, of Charles Baudelaire and Huysmans. There is an untranslatable English epithet, the epithet "uncanny," to denote supernatural horror; that epithet (*unheimlich* in German) is applicable to certain pages of *Vathek*, but not, as far as I recall, to any other book before it.

Chapman indicates some of the books that influenced Beckford: the *Bibliothèque Orientale*, by Barthélemy d'Herbelot; the *Quatre Facardins*, by Hamilton; *La princesse de Babylone*, by Voltaire; the always reviled and admirable *Mille et une Nuits*, by Galland. To that list I would add the *Carceri d'invenzione*, by Piranesi: etchings praised by Beckford, depicting mighty palaces which are also inextricable labyrinths. In the first chapter of *Vathek*, Beckford enumerates five palaces dedicated to the five senses; in the *Adone*, Marino had already described five analogous gardens.

William Beckford required only three days and two nights in the winter of 1782 to write the tragic history of his caliph. He wrote it in French; Henley translated it into English in 1785. The original is unfaithful to the translation; Saintsbury observes that eighteenth-century French is less apt than English to communicate the "undefined horrors" (the phrase is Beckford's) of the very unusual story.

The Everyman's Library published Henley's English version. Perrin, of Paris, has published the original text, revised and prefaced by Mallarmé. It is strange that Chapman's laborious bibliography does not mention that revision and that preface.

Buenos Aires, 1943

140

About *The Purple Land*

This novel, Hudson's first, is reducible to a formula so ancient that it can almost comprise the *Odyssey*; so fundamental that the name formula subtly defames and degrades it. The hero begins his wandering, and his adventures encounter him along the way. *The Golden Ass* and the fragments of the *Satyricon* belong to this nomadic, random genre, as do *Pickwick* and *Don Quixote*, *Kim* of Lahore and *Segundo Sombra* of Areco. I do not believe there is any justification for calling those books picaresque novels: first, because of the unfavorable connotation of the term; second, because of its local and temporal limitations (Spain, sixteenth and seventeenth centuries). Further, the genre is complex. Disorder, incoherence, and variety are not inaccessible, but they must be governed by a secret order, which is revealed by degrees. I have recalled several famous examples; perhaps all show obvious defects.

Cervantes utilizes two types of characters: an emaciated, tall, ascetic, mad, and grandiloquent nobleman; a corpulent, short, gluttonous, sane, and colloquial peasant. That very symmetrical and persistent disharmony finally deprives them of reality, lowers them to the stature of circus figures. (In the seventh chapter of *El Payador* our own Lugones already insinuated that reproach.) Kipling invents Kim, the little friend of the whole world, who is completely free: a few chapters later, impelled by some sort of patriotic perversion, he

141

gives him the horrible occupation of a spy. (In his literary autobiography, written about thirty-five years later, Kipling shows that he is impenitent and even unaware of the implications.) I note those defects without animadversion; I do it to judge *The Purple Land* with equal sincerity.

The most elementary of the sort of novels I am considering aim at a mere succession of adventures, mere variety: the seven voyages of Sinbad the Sailor are perhaps the best example, for the hero is just an underling, as impersonal and passive as the reader. In other novels (which are scarcely more complex) the function of the events is to reveal the hero's character, and even his absurdities and manias; that is the case in the first part of *Don Quixote*. In others (which correspond to a later stage) the movement is dual, reciprocal; the hero changes the circumstances, the circumstances change the hero's character. That is the case with the second part of the *Quixote*, with Mark Twain's *Huckleberry Finn*, with *The Purple Land*. The latter actually has two plots. The first, the visible one: the adventures of the young Englishman Richard Lamb in the Banda Oriental. The second, the intimate, invisible one: the assimilation of Lamb, his gradual conversion to a barbarous morality that reminds one of Rousseau a little and anticipates Nietzsche a little. His *Wanderjahre* are also *Lehrjahre*. Hudson was personally acquainted with the rigors of a semibarbarous, pastoral life; Rousseau and Nietzsche knew such a life only through the sedentary volumes of the *Histoire Générale des Voyages* and the Homeric epics. The foregoing statement does not mean that *The Purple Land* is flawless. It suffers from an obvious defect, which may logically be attributed to the hazards of improvisation: the vain and tedious complexity of certain adventures. I am thinking of the ones near the end of the book: they are so complicated that they weary the attention, but do not hold it. In those onerous chapters Hudson appears not to understand that the book is successive (almost as purely successive as the *Satyricon* or the *Buscón*) and benumbs it with useless artifices. This is a common mistake; for example, Dickens tends toward similar prolixities in all his novels.

The Purple Land is perhaps unexcelled by any work of Gaucho literature. It would be deplorable if we let a certain topographical

142

confusion and three or four errors or errata (*Camelones* for *Cane-lones, Aria* for *Arias, Gumesinda* for *Gumersinda*) conceal that truth from us. *The Purple Land* is essentially Creole, native to South America. The fact that the narrator is an Englishman justifies certain explanations and certain emphases required by his readers, which would be anomalous in a Gaucho accustomed to such things. In Number 31 of *Sur*, Ezequiel Martínez Estrada wrote:

Never before has there been a poet, a painter, or an interpreter of things Argentine like Hudson, nor will there ever be again. Hernández is one part of the cosmorama of our life that Hudson sang, described, and explained . . . The final pages of *The Purple Land* express the maximum philosophy and the supreme justification of America in the face of Western civilization and the refinements of culture.

As we see, Martínez Estrada did not hesitate to prefer Hudson's total output to the most notable of the canonical books of our Gaucho literature. Incomparably more vast is the scope of *The Purple Land*. The *Martín Fierro* (notwithstanding the canonization proposed by Lugones) is less the epic of our origins—in 1872!—than the auto-biography of a cutthroat, adulterated by bravado and lamentation that seem to prophesy the tango. Ascasubi's work is more vivid, it has more joy, more passion, but those traits are fragmentary and secret in three incidental volumes of four hundred pages each. In spite of the variety of its dialogues, *Don Segundo Sombra* is marred by the propensity to exaggerate the most innocent tasks. No one is unaware that the narrator is a Gaucho; and therefore to indulge in the kind of dramatic hyperbole that converts the herding of bulls into an exploit of war is doubly unjustified. Güiraldes assumes an air of solemnity when he relates the everyday work of the country. Hudson (like Ascasubi, like Hernández, like Eduardo Gutiérrez) describes with complete naturalness events that may even be atrocious.

Someone will observe that in *The Purple Land* the Gaucho has only a lateral, secondary role. So much the better for the accuracy of the portrayal, we reply. The Gaucho is a taciturn man, the Gaucho does not know, or he scorns, the complex delights of memory and introspection. To depict him as autobiographical and effusive is to deform him.

143

Another of Hudson's adroit strokes is his treatment of geography. Born in the Province of Buenos Aires in the magic circle of the pampa, he nonetheless chooses to write about the purple land where the revolutionary horsemen used their first and last lances: the Banda Oriental. Gauchos from the Province of Buenos Aires are the rule in Argentine literature: the paradoxical reason for that is the existence of a large city, Buenos Aires, the point of origin of famous writers of Gaucho literature. If we look to history instead of to literature, we shall see that the glorification of the Gaucho has had but little influence on the destinies of their province, and none on the destinies of their country. The typical organism of Gaucho warfare, the revolutionary horseman, appears in Buenos Aires only sporadically. The authority falls to the city, to the leaders of the city. Only rarely does some individual—Hormiga Negra in legal documents, Martín Fierro in literature—attain, with the rebellion of a fugitive, a certain notoriety with the police.

As I have said, Hudson selects the Banda Oriental as the setting for his hero's escapades. That propitious choice permits him to enlist chance and the diversification of war to enrich Richard Lamb's destiny—and chance favors the opportunities for vagabond love. Macaulay, in the article about Bunyan, marveled that one man's imaginings would become, years later, the personal memories of many other men. Hudson's imaginings remain in the memory: British bullets that resound in the Paysandú night; the oblivious Gaucho who enjoys his smoke of strong tobacco before the battle; the girl who surrenders to a stranger on the secret shore of a river.

Improving the perfection of a phrase divulged by Boswell, Hudson says that many times in his life he undertook the study of metaphysics, but happiness always interrupted him. That sentence (one of the most memorable I have encountered in literature) is typical of the man and the book. In spite of the bloodshed and the separations, *The Purple Land* is one of the very few happy books in the world. (Another, which also is about America, also nearly paradisaic in tone, is Mark Twain's *Huckleberry Finn*.) I am not thinking of the chaotic debate between pessimists and optimists; I am not thinking of the doctrinal happiness the pathetic Whitman inexorably imposed on himself; I am thinking of the happy disposition of Richard

Lamb, of the hospitality with which he welcomed every vicissitude of life, whether bitter or sweet.

One last observation. To perceive or not to perceive the Creole nuances may be quite unimportant, but the fact is that of all the foreigners (not, of course, excluding the Spaniards) no one perceives them like the Englishman—Miller, Robertson, Burton, Cunningham Grahame, Hudson.

Buenos Aires, 1941

From Someone to Nobody

In the beginning, God is the Gods (Elohim), a plural that some say denotes majesty and others say denotes plenitude and in which some have thought they observed an echo of earlier polytheisms or a prefiguring of the doctrine, declared in Nicaea, that God is One and is Three. Elohim is used with a singular verb; the first verse of the Law says literally: "In the beginning the Gods created the heaven and the earth"—the verb *created* is in the singular. Despite the vagueness suggested by the plural, Elohim is concrete; God is called Jehovah and we read that He walked in the garden in the air of the day, or, as the English versions say, "in the cool of the day." Human qualities define Him; in one part of the Scripture we read: "And it repented Jehovah that He had made man on the earth, and it grieved Him at His heart; and in another, "For I the Lord thy God am a jealous God"; and in another, "In the fire of My wrath have I spoken." The subject of those locutions is indisputably Someone, a corporal Someone Whom the centuries will continue to depict and magnify. His titles vary: The Mighty One of Jacob, the Holy One of Israel, I Am That I Am, God of the Armies, King of Kings. The last, which was no doubt the inspiration (by opposition) of the Servant of the Servants of God of Gregory the Great, is a superlative of king in the original text: as Fray Luis de

146

León writes, "It is a property of the Hebrew language to use the same word twice for the sake of emphasis, either favorable or unfavorable. And so, to say 'Song of Songs' is the same as saying 'Song among Songs,' 'he is a man among men,' that is, famous and eminent among all men and more excellent than many others." In the first centuries of our era theologians supply the prefix *omni*, which was previously reserved for adjectives describing nature or Jupiter. They coin words like "omnipotent," "omnipresent," "omniscient," which make of God a respectful chaos of unimaginable superlatives. That nomenclature, like the others, seems to limit the divinity: at the end of the fifth century the obscure author of the *Corpus Dionysiacum* declares that no affirmative predicate is fitting for God. Nothing should be affirmed of Him, everything can be denied. Schopenhauer notes dryly: "That theology is the only true one, but it has no content." Written in Greek, the tracts and letters of the *Corpus Dionysiacum* encounter a reader in the ninth century who puts them into Latin: Johannes Erigena or Scotus, or rather John the Irishman, whose name in history is Scotus Erigena or Irish Irish. He formulates a doctrine of a pantheistic nature: particular things are theophanies (revelations or appearances of the divine) and behind them is God, the only reality, "who does not know what He is, because He is not a what, and is incomprehensible to Himself and to all intelligence." He is not sapient, He is more than sapient; He is not good, He is more than good; inscrutably He exceeds and rejects all attributes. John the Irishman, to define Him, utilized the word *nihilum*, which is nothingness; God is the primordial nothingness of the *creatio ex nihilo*, the abyss where first the archetypes and then concrete beings were engendered. He is Nothing and Nobody; those who imagined Him thus did so in the belief that it was more than being a Who, more than being a What. Analogously, Shankara teaches that men in a deep sleep are the universe, are God.

The process I have just illustrated is not, certainly, aleatory. Magnification to nothingness occurs or tends to occur in all cults; unequivocally we observe it in the case of Shakespeare. His contemporary, Ben Jonson, loves him without reaching the point of idolatry, "on this side Idolatry"; Dryden declares that he is the Homer of the dramatic poets of England, but admits that he is often insipid and pompous; the discursive eighteenth century seeks to appraise his virtues and to rebuke his faults; in 1774, Maurice Morgan states that King Lear and Falstaff are nothing but modifications of the mind of their inventor; at the beginning of the nineteenth century that opinion is re-created by Coleridge, for whom Shakespeare is no longer a man but a literary variation of the infinite God of Spinoza. Coleridge wrote that Shakespeare was a *natura naturata*, an effect, but that the universal, potentially present in the particular, was revealed to him—not as abstracted from the observation of a plurality of cases but rather as the substance capable of infinite modifications, of which his personal existence was only one. Hazlitt corroborated or confirmed that, and said that Shakespeare was like other men in every way except in being like other men; and that intimately he was nothing, but he was everything that others were, or could be. Later Hugo compared him to the ocean, the possible forms of which were infinite.[1]

To be one thing is inexorably not to be all the other things. The confused intuition of that truth has induced men to imagine that not being is more than being something and that, somehow, not to be is to be everything. That fallacy is inherent in the words of the legendary king of Hindustan who renounces power and goes out to beg in the streets: "From this day forward I have no realm or my realm is limitless, from this day forward my body does not belong to me or all the earth belongs to me." Schopenhauer has written that history is an interminable and perplexing dream of human generations; in the dream there are recurring forms, perhaps nothing but forms; one of them is the process described in this essay.

Buenos Aires, 1950

[1] The image is repeated in Buddhism. The first texts relate that the Buddha, under the fig tree, perceives by intuition the infinite concatenation of all the causes and effects of the universe, the past and future incarnations of each being. The last texts, written centuries later, reason that nothing is real and that all knowledge is fictitious and that if there were as many Ganges Rivers as there are grains of sand in the Ganges and again as many Ganges Rivers as grains of sand in those new Ganges Rivers, the number of grains of sand would be smaller than the number of things *not known* by the Buddha.

148

Forms of a Legend

People find it repugnant to see an aged person, an invalid, or a dead body, and yet all are subject to old age, illness, and death; the Buddha declared that this thought induced him to leave his home and parents and to don the yellow robe of the ascetics. The testimony is in one of the books of the canon. Another book records the parable of the five secret messengers sent by the gods: a child, a stooped old man, a paralytic, a criminal on the rack, and a corpse, who tell him that it is our destiny to be born, to grow old, to suffer, to endure just punishment, and to die. The Judge of the Shadows (in the myths of India, Yama has that role because he was the first man who died) asks the sinner if he has seen the messengers. He admits that he has, but he has not deciphered their message; the guards imprison him in a house filled with fire. Perhaps the Buddha did not invent that ominous parable. We are satisfied with the knowledge that he said it (*Majjhima-nikāya*, 130) and that he never, perhaps, related it to his own life.

Reality may be too complex for oral transmission. Legends recreate it in a way that is only accidentally false and permits it to travel through the world from mouth to mouth. An old man, a sick man, and a dead man appear in both the parable and the declaration. Time made the two texts into one and in welding them together fashioned a new story.

149

Siddhartha, the Bodhisattva, the pre-Buddha, is the son of a great king, Suddhodana, of the lineage of the sun. On the night of his conception, his mother dreams that a white elephant with six tusks comes to her and touches her right side.[1] The sages prophesy that her son will reign over the world or will make the wheel of doctrine turn,[2] and will teach men how to free themselves from life and death. The king, who prefers to have Siddhartha attain temporal and not eternal grandeur, shuts him up in a palace divested of all the things that may show him he is corruptible. And thus he spends twenty-nine years of illusory happiness dedicated to sensual pleasures. One morning Siddhartha rides out in his chariot and sees with amazement a stooped man, "whose hair is not like other men's, whose body is not like other men's," who leans on a cane to be able to walk and whose body trembles. He asks about the man's identity; the chariot driver explains that he is an old man, and that all the men on earth will be like him one day. Uneasily, Siddhartha orders his driver to return home at once, but on another outing he sees a man wasted by fever, teeming with leprosy and ulcers; the driver explains that he is a sick man, and that no one is exempt from that danger. On another outing he sees a man borne on a bier; that inert figure is a dead man, they tell him, and to die is the rule for everyone who is born. On another outing, the last one, he sees a monk of the mendicant order who desires neither to live nor to die. Peace is on his face; Siddhartha has found the way.

Hardy (*Der Buddhismus nach älteren Pali-Werken*) praised the

---

[1] For us, this dream is a mere ugliness, but not to the Hindus. The elephant, a domestic animal, is the symbol of mansuetude. The multiplication of tusks cannot be disturbing to the spectators of an art that, to suggest that God is everything, creates figures with multiple arms and faces. Six is the usual number (six ways of transmigration; six Buddhas anterior to the Buddha; six cardinal points, counting the zenith and the nadir; six divinities which the Yajur-Veda calls the six doors of Brahma).

[2] This metaphor may have suggested to the Tibetans the invention of the prayer machines, wheels or cylinders that revolve around an axis, filled with strips of rolled paper on which magic words are repeated. Some of the machines are manually operated; others are like large mills and are moved by water or the wind.

150

color of that legend. A contemporary Indologist, A. Foucher (whose tone of mockery is not always intelligent or urbane) writes that, granted the Bodhisattva's previous ignorance, the story has both dramatic climax and philosophical import. At the beginning of the fifth century the monk Fa-Hien made a pilgrimage to the kingdoms of Hindustan in search of sacred books, and saw the ruins of the city of Kapilavastu with the four images that Asoka erected at the north, south, east, and west of the walls to commemorate the encounters of Siddhartha. At the beginning of the seventh century a Christian monk wrote the novel entitled *Barlaam and Josaphat*. Josaphat (Joasaf, Bodhisattva) is the son of a king of India. The astrologers predict that he will reign over a larger kingdom, the Kingdom of Glory. The king confines him in a palace, but Josaphat discovers the unfortunate condition of men in the guise of a blind man, a leper, and a dying man. In the end he is converted to the faith by the hermit Barlaam. This Christian version of the legend was translated into many languages, including Dutch and Latin; at the request of Hakon Hakonarson, a *Barlaams Saga* was produced in Iceland around the middle of the thirteenth century. Cardinal César Baronio included Josaphat in his revision (1585–1590) of the Roman Martyrology. In 1615, in his continuation of the *Décadas*, Diego de Couto reported the similarity of the spurious Indian fable to the true and pious history of St. Josaphat. The reader will find that and much more in the first volume of *Orígenes de la Novela* by Menéndez y Pelayo.

The legend that in Western countries determined the Buddha's canonization by Rome had, withal, one defect: the encounters it postulates are effective but they are also incredible. Four outings of Siddhartha and four didactic figures do not coincide with the uses of chance. Less attentive to the aesthetic than to the conversion of souls, the doctors tried to justify that anomaly; Koeppen (*Die Religion des Buddha*, I, 82) notes that in the last form of the legend, the leper, the dead man, and the monk are illusions produced by the divinities to instruct Siddhartha. And so in the third book of the Sanskrit epic *Buddhacarita* one reads that the gods created a dead man, and as they carried him only the chariot driver and the prince saw him. In

151

a legendary biography from the sixteenth century, the four apparitions are four metamorphoses of a god (Wieger: *Vies chinoises du
Bouddha*, 37–41).

The *Lalitavistara* had gone even further. On the pages of that compilation of prose and verse, written in an impure Sanskrit, the history
of the Redeemer is so inflated that it becomes oppressive and bewildering. The Buddha, surrounded by twelve thousand monks and
thirty-two thousand Bodhisattvas, reveals the text of the work to the
gods. From the fourth heaven he established the period, the conti-
nent, the kingdom, and the caste into which he would be reborn to
die for the last time. (The words of his speech are uttered to the
accompaniment of eighty thousand kettledrums; his mother's body
is filled with the strength of ten thousand elephants.) In the strange
poem the Buddha directs each stage of his destiny; he causes the
divinities to project the four symbolic figures and, when he interrogates the chariot driver, he already knows who they are and what
they mean. Foucher sees this as mere servility on the part of the
authors, who cannot tolerate the thought that the Buddha does not
know what a servant knows. To my mind, the enigma deserves another solution. The Buddha creates the images and then interrogates
a third party about their meaning. Theologically it would perhaps
be possible to answer: the book is of the Mahayana school, which
teaches that the temporal Buddha is the emanation or reflection of an
eternal Buddha; the Buddha of heaven orders events, the earthly
Buddha suffers them or executes them. (With another mythology or
vocabulary, our century speaks of the unconscious.) The humanity
of the Son, the second person of God, was able to shout from the
Cross: "My God, my God, why hast thou forsaken me?"; similarly,
the Buddha's humanity was capable of horror at the forms his own
divinity had created. Such dogmatic subtleties are not indispensable
for a solution of the problem. It suffices to remember that all the
religions of India and in particular Buddhism teach that the world is
illusory. "The minute narration of the game" (of a Buddha) is what
Lalitavistara means, according to Winternitz; a game or a dream is,
for the Mahayana, the life of the Buddha on earth, which is another
dream. Siddhartha chooses his nation and his parents, Siddhartha
fashions four forms that will overwhelm him with consternation,

152

Siddhartha orders that another form shall declare the meaning of the first forms—all of which is reasonable if we think of it as a dream of Siddhartha. Or, even better, if we think of it as a dream in which Siddhartha figures (as the leper and the monk figure) and as a dream which no one actually dreams—because to the Northern school[3] of Buddhism the world and the proselytes and Nirvana and the wheel of transmigrations and the Buddha are equally unreal. No one is extinguished in Nirvana, we read in a famous treatise, because the extinction of incommensurable, innumerable beings in Nirvana is like the disappearance of a phantasmagoria created by a sorcerer's magic; and elsewhere it is written that everything is mere emptiness, mere name, including the book that declares it and the man who reads it. Paradoxically, the numerical excesses of the poem subtract, rather than add, reality; twelve thousand monks and thirty-two thousand Bodhisattvas are less concrete than *one* monk and *one* Bodhisattva. The vast forms and the vast numbers (Chapter XII includes a series of twenty-three words that indicate the unit followed by an increasing number of zeros, from 9 to 49, 51 and 53) are monstrous bubbles, emphases of Nothingness. And so the unreal has continually made inroads in the story; first it gave a fantastic character to the figures, then to the prince, and, with the prince, to all the generations and to the universe.

At the end of the nineteenth century Oscar Wilde proposed a variation. The happy prince dies in the seclusion of the palace, without having discovered sorrow, but his posthumous effigy discerns it from atop his pedestal.

The chronology of India is uncertain; my erudition is even more unreliable. Koeppen and Hermann Beckh are perhaps as fallible as the compiler who has hazarded this article. It would not surprise me if my history of the legend turned out to be legendary, formed of substantial truth and accidental errors.

[3] Rhys Davids proscribes the locution "Northern school," which was introduced by Burnouf, but its use in this sentence is less onerous than Great Crossing or Great Vehicle, which would have given the reader pause.

From Allegories to Novels

For all of us, the allegory is an aesthetic error. (My first impulse was to write "the allegory is nothing more than an error of aesthetics," but then I noticed that an allegory had crept into my sentence.) To the best of my knowledge, the allegorical genre has been analyzed by Schopenhauer (*Welt als Wille und Vorstellung*, I, 50), by De Quincey (*Writings*, XI, 198), by Francesco De Sanctis (*Storia della letteratura italiana*, VII), by Croce (*Estetica*, 39), and by Chesterton (*G. F. Watts*, 83). In this essay I shall consider only the last two. Croce denies the allegorical art; Chesterton vindicates it. I agree with the former, but I should like to know how a form we consider unjustifiable could have enjoyed so much favor.

Croce's words are crystalline; let me repeat them now:

If the symbol is conceived as inseparable from the artistic intuition, it is a synonym of the intuition itself, which always has an ideal character. If the symbol is conceived as separable, if the symbol can be expressed on the one hand and the thing symbolized can be expressed on the other, one falls back into the intellectualist error. The supposed symbol is the exposition of an abstract concept; it is an allegory; it is science, or art that copies science. But in fairness we must point out that in some cases the allegory is innocuous. A moral of sorts can be educed from the *Jerusalén libertada*; and from the *Adone* by Marino, the poet of lust, the

154

reflection that unbridled pleasure will end in pain. The sculptor can place a card on a statue saying that it is Clemency or Kindness. Allegories of this sort added to a finished work have no adverse effect on it. They are expressions added extrinsically to other expressions. A page in prose that relates another thought of the poet is added to the *Jerusalén*; a verse or stanza that tells what the poet wishes to convey is added to the *Adone*. The word "clemency" or the word "kindness" is added to the statue.

On page 222 of the book *La poesia* (Bari, 1946) the tone is more hostile: "The allegory is not a direct mode of spiritual manifestation, but rather a kind of writing or cryptography."

Croce does not admit any difference between the content and the form. The latter is the former and the former is the latter. The allegory seems monstrous to him because it aspires to encipher two contents in one form: the immediate or literal one (Dante, guided by Virgil, comes to Beatrice) and the figurative one (man finally comes to faith, guided by reason). He believes that this way of writing fosters tedious enigmas.

To vindicate the allegory, Chesterton begins by denying that language is the only way to express reality.

Man knows that there are in the soul tints more bewildering, more numberless, and more nameless than the colours of an autumn forest; . . . Yet he seriously believes that these things can every one of them, in all their tones and semi-tones, in all their blends and unions, be accurately represented by an arbitrary system of grunts and squeals. He believes that an ordinary civilized stockbroker can really produce out of his own inside noises which denote all the mysteries of memory and all the agonies of desire.

With one form of communication declared to be insufficient, there is room for others; allegory may be one of them, like architecture or music. It is made up of words, but it is not a language of language, a sign of other signs. For example, Beatrice is not a sign of the word *faith*; she is a sign of active virtue and the secret illuminations that this word indicates—a more precise sign, a richer and happier sign than the monosyllable *faith*.

I am not certain which of the eminent contradictors is right. I know that at one time the allegorical art was considered quite charm-

155

ing (the labyrinthine *Roman de la Rose*, which survives in two hundred manuscripts, consists of twenty-four thousand verses) and is now intolerable. We feel that, besides being intolerable, it is stupid and frivolous. Neither Dante, who told the story of his passion in the *Vita nuova*; nor the Roman Boethius, writing his *De consolatione* in the tower of Pavia, in the shadow of his executioner's sword, would have understood our feeling. How can I explain that difference in outlook without simply appealing to the principle of changing tastes?

Coleridge observes that all men are born Aristotelian or Platonist. The latter know by intuition that ideas are realities; the former, that they are generalizations; for the latter, language is nothing but a system of arbitrary symbols; for the former, it is the map of the universe. The Platonist knows that the universe is somehow a cosmos, an order, which, for the Aristotelian, may be an error or a figment of our partial knowledge. Across the latitudes and the ages, the two immortal antagonists change their name and language: one is Parmenides, Plato, Spinoza, Kant, Francis Bradley; the other is Heraclitus, Aristotle, Locke, Hume, William James. In the arduous schools of the Middle Ages they all invoke Aristotle, the master of human reason (*Convivio*, IV, 2), but the nominalists are Aristotle; the realists, Plato. George Henry Lewes has observed that the only medieval debate of any philosophical value is the debate between nominalism and realism. This opinion is rather temerarious, but it emphasizes the importance of the persistent controversy provoked at the beginning of the ninth century by a sentence from Porphyry, which Boethius translated and annotated; a controversy that Anselm and Roscellinus continued at the end of the eleventh century and that William of Occam reanimated in the fourteenth.

As might be supposed, the passage of so many years multiplied the intermediate positions and the distinctions to the point of infinity. Nevertheless, for realism the universals (Plato would say the ideas, forms; we call them abstract concepts) were fundamental; and for nominalism, the individuals. The history of philosophy is not a vain museum of distractions and verbal games; the two theses probably correspond to two manners of intuitively perceiving reality. Maurice de Wulf writes: "Ultrarealism gained the first adherents. The chronicler Heriman (eleventh century) speaks of those who teach dialectic

156

in re as 'antiqui doctores'; Abelard calls dialectic an 'ancient doctrine,' and the name of 'moderni' is applied to its adversaries until the end of the twelfth century." A thesis that is inconceivable now seemed obvious in the ninth century, and it somehow endured until the fourteenth century. Nominalism, which was formerly the novelty of a few, encompasses everyone today; its victory is so vast and fundamental that its name is unnecessary. No one says that he is a nominalist, because nobody is anything else. But we must try to understand that for the people of the Middle Ages reality was not men but humanity, not the individuals but mankind, not the species but the genus, not the genera but God. I believe that allegorical literature has developed from such concepts (of which the clearest manifestation is perhaps the quadruple system of Erigena). The allegory is a fable of abstractions, as the novel is a fable of individuals. The abstractions are personified; therefore, in every allegory there is something of the novel. The individuals proposed by novelists aspire to be generic (Dupin is Reason, Don Segundo Sombra is the Gaucho); an allegorical element inheres in novels.

The passage from the allegory to the novel, from the species to the individual, from realism to nominalism, required several centuries, but I shall attempt to suggest an ideal date when it occurred. That day in 1382 when Geoffrey Chaucer, who perhaps did not believe he was a nominalist, wished to translate a line from Boccaccio into English, *E con gli occulti ferri i Tradimenti* ("And Treachery with hidden weapons"), and he said it like this: "The smyler with the knyf under the cloke." The original is in the seventh book of the *Teseide*; the English version, in "The Knightes Tale."

Buenos Aires, 1949

The Innocence of Layamon

Legouis has seen the paradox of Layamon but not, I believe, his pathos. The introduction to the *Brut,* written in the third person at the beginning of the thirteenth century, contains the facts of his life. Layamon wrote:

There was in the land a priest named Layamon; he was the son of Leovenath (may God have mercy on his soul!), and he lived in Ernley in a noble church on the banks of the Severn, a good place to be. He hit upon the idea of relating the exploits of the Englishmen, what they were named and where they came from and which ones arrived on English soil after the flood. Layamon traveled throughout the land and acquired the noble books that were his models. He took the English book made by St. Bede; he took another in Latin made by St. Albin and St. Augustine, who brought us the faith; he took a third and placed it in the middle, the work of a French cleric named Wace, who knew how to write well, and gave it to the noble Leonor, queen of the great Henry. Layamon opened those three books and turned the pages; he looked at them lovingly—may God have mercy on him!—and picked up the pen and wrote on parchment and summoned the right words and made the three books into one. Now Layamon, for the love of God Omnipotent, begs those who read this book and learn the truths it teaches to pray for the soul of his father, who begot him, and for the soul of his mother, who bore him, and for his own soul, to make it better. Amen.

Thirty thousand irregular verses proceed to recount the battles of the Britons and especially of Arthur against the Picts, the Norse, and the Saxons.

The first impression, and perhaps the last, given by Layamon's introduction is of infinite, almost incredible, simplicity. The childish habit of saying *Layamon* and not *I* enhances that impression, but behind the candid words the emotion is complex. Layamon is touched not only by the subject matter of the songs, but also by the somewhat magical circumstance of seeing himself singing them; this reciprocity corresponds to the "Illo Virgilium me tempore" of the *Georgics* or to the beautiful "Ego ille qui quondam" that someone prefaced to the *Aeneid*.

A legend picked up by Dionysius of Halicarnassus and adopted famously by Virgil states that Rome was founded by men of the race of Aeneas, the Trojan who battles Achilles on the pages of the *Iliad*. Similarly a *Historia Regum Britanniae* dating from the beginning of the twelfth century attributes the founding of London ("citie that some tyme cleped was New Troy") to a great-grandson of Aeneas called Brutus, whose name would be perpetuated in Britannia. Brutus is the first king in the secular chronicle of Layamon; he is followed by others, who have known a very diverse fortune in literature: Hudibras, Lear, Gorboduc, Ferrex and Porrex, Lud, Cymbeline, Vortigern, Uther Pendragon (Uther Dragon's Head), and Arthur of the Round Table, "the king who was and will be," as his mysterious epitaph says. Arthur is mortally wounded in his last battle; but Merlin, who in the *Brut* is not the son of the Devil but the son of a silent phantom of gold loved by his mother in dreams, prophesies that he will return (like Barbarossa) when his people need him. The restless hordes, the "pagan dogs" of Hengest (the Saxons who were scattered over the face of England from the fifth century onward) wage war against him in vain.

It has been said that Layamon was the first of the English poets; it is more correct and more poignant to think of him as the last of the Saxon poets. The latter, converted to the faith of Jesus, applied the harsh accent and the military images of the Germanic epics to that new mythology (in one of the poems of Cynewulf, the Twelve Apostles resist the onrush of swords and are skilled in the manipula-

159

tion of shields; in the Exodus, the Israelites who cross the Red Sea are Vikings); Layamon subjected the courtly and magical fictions of the *Matière de Bretagne* to that same rigor. Because of the subject, he is one of the many poets of the Breton Cycle, a distant colleague of that anonymous writer who revealed to Francesca da Rimini and to Paolo the love they felt for each other without knowing it. In spirit he is a lineal descendant of those Saxon rhapsodists who reserved their felicitous words for the description of battles and who did not produce a single amatory stanza in four centuries. Layamon has forgotten the metaphors of his ancestors; in the *Brut*, the sea is not the whale's path, nor are the arrows vipers of war, but the vision of the world is the same. Like Stevenson, like Flaubert, like so many men of letters, the sedentary cleric takes pleasure in verbal violence; where Wace wrote, "On that day the Britons killed Passent and the Irish King," Layamon amplifies:

And Uther the Good said these words: "Passent, here you will remain, for here comes Uther on his horse!" He hit him on his head and knocked him down and put his sword in his mouth (giving him a food that was new to him) and the point of the sword disappeared into the ground. Then Uther said: "Now it is well with you, Irishman; all England is yours. I deliver it into your hands so that you may stay here and live with us. Look, here it is; now you will have it forever."

In every line of Anglo-Saxon verse there are certain words, two in the first half and one in the second, that begin with the same consonant or with a vowel. Layamon tries to observe that old metrical law, but the coupled octosyllables of the *Geste des Bretons* by Wace—one of the three "noble books"—continually distract him with the new temptation to rhyme, and so after *brother* we have *other* and *night* after *light*. The Norman Conquest took place around the middle of the eleventh century. The *Brut* dates from the beginning of the thirteenth, but the vocabulary of the poem is almost purely Germanic; there are not fifty words of French origin in thirty thousand verses. Here is a passage that is scarcely a prefiguring of the English language and has notable affinities with the German:

And seothe ich cumen wulle
to mine kineriche
and wunien mid Brutten
mid muchelere wunne.

Those were Arthur's last words. Their meaning is: "And then I shall go to my kingdom and I shall dwell among Britons with great delight."

Layamon sang with fervor about the ancient battles of the Britons against the Saxon invaders, as if he were not a Saxon and as if Britons and Saxons had not been, since Hastings, conquered by the Normans. The fact is singular and permits several conjectures. Layamon, son of Leovenath (Leofnoth), lived not far from Wales, the bulwark of the Celts and the source (according to Gaston Paris) of the complex myth of Arthur; his mother could very well have been a Briton. This is a likely conjecture, but it cannot be verified, and it is perhaps not very significant; one could also suppose that the poet was the son and grandson of Saxons, but that intimately the *jus soli* was stronger than the *jus sanguinis.* Not so dissimilar is the case of the Argentine with no Querendí blood who habitually identifies himself with the Indian defenders of his land rather than with the Spaniards of Cabrera or Juan de Garay. Another possibility is that Layamon, perhaps unwittingly, gave the Britons of the *Brut* the value of Saxons, and the Saxons the value of Normans. The enigmas, the *Bestiary,* and the curious runes of Cynewulf prove that such cryptographic or allegorical exercises were not alien to that ancient literature; but something tells me that this speculation is fantastic. If Layamon had thought that the conquerors of yesterday were the conquered of today, and the conquerors of today could be the conquered of tomorrow, I believe he would have utilized the simile of the Wheel of Fortune, which appears in the *De Consolatione;* or he would have had recourse to the prophetic books of the Bible, not to the intricate romance of Arthur.

The subjects of the earlier epics were the exploits of a hero or the loyalty that warriors owe to their captain; the real subject of the *Brut* is England. Layamon could not foresee that two centuries after

161

his death his alliteration would be ridiculous ("I can not geste—rum, ram, ruf—by lettre," says a character in Chaucer) and his language, a rustic jargon. He could not suspect that his insults to the Saxons of Hengest were the last words in the Saxon language, destined to die and to be born again in the English language. According to the Germanist Ker, he scarcely knew the literature whose tradition he inherited; he knew nothing of the wanderings of Widsith among Persians and Hebrews nor of the combat of Beowulf in the bottom of the red marsh. He knew nothing of the great verses from which his own were to spring; perhaps he would not have understood them. His curious isolation, his solitude, make him, now, pathetic. *"No one knows who he is,"* said León Bloy. Of that intimate ignorance no symbol is better than this forgotten man, who abhorred his Saxon heritage with Saxon vigor, and who was the last Saxon poet and never knew it.

For Bernard Shaw

At the end of the thirteenth century Raymond Lully (Ramon Lull) attempted to solve all the mysteries by means of a frame with unequal, revolving, concentric disks, subdivided into sectors with Latin words. At the beginning of the nineteenth century John Stuart Mill expressed the fear that the number of musical combinations would some day be exhausted and that the future would hold no place for new Webers and Mozarts. At the end of the nineteenth century Kurd Lasswitz played with the overwhelming fantasy of a universal library that would record all the variations of the twenty-odd orthographic symbols, or rather everything that can be expressed, in all the languages of the world. Lull's machine, Mill's fear, and Lasswitz's chaotic library may make us laugh, but they merely exaggerate a common propensity to consider metaphysics and the arts as a sort of combinatory game. Those who play that game forget that a book is more than a verbal structure, or a series of verbal structures; a book is the dialogue with the reader, and the peculiar accent he gives to its voice, and the changing and durable images it leaves in his memory. That dialogue is infinite. Now the words *amica silentia lunae* mean "the intimate, silent, and shining moon," and in the *Aeneid* they meant the interlunar period, the darkness that per-

163

mitted the Greeks to enter the citadel of Troy.[1] Literature is not exhaustible, for the sufficient and simple reason that a single book is not. A book is not an isolated entity: it is a narration, an axis of innumerable narrations. One literature differs from another, either before or after it, not so much because of the text as for the manner in which it is read. If I were able to read any contemporary page—this one, for example—as it would be read in the year 2000, I would know what literature would be like in the year 2000. The concept of literature as a formal game leads, in the best of cases, to the good work of the period and the strophe, to a proper craftsman (Johnson, Renan, Flaubert), and in the worst of cases, to the vexations of a work formed of surprises dictated by vanity and chance (Gracián, Herrera Reissig).

If literature were nothing but verbal algebra, anyone could produce any book simply by practicing variations. The lapidary formula *Everything flows* abbreviates the philosophy of Heraclitus in two words. Raymond Lully would tell us that, after saying the first word, one needs only to substitute intransitive verbs in order to discover the second word and to obtain, by a methodical chance, that philosophy and many, many more. But we would reply that the formula obtained by elimination would lack value and even meaning. If it is to have any virtue we must conceive it as Heraclitus did, as an experience of Heraclitus, although "Heraclitus" is only the presumable subject of that experience. I said that a book is a dialogue, a form of narration. In the dialogue an interlocutor is not the sum total or the intermediate value of what he says: it is possible for him not to speak and yet to reveal intelligence, or to emit intelligent observations and still reveal stupidity. The same occurs with literature. D'Artagnan

---

[1] That is how Milton and Dante interpreted those words, to judge by certain passages which seem imitative. In the *Comedy* (*Inferno*, I, 60; V, 28) we have *d'ogni luce muto* and *dove il sol tace* to indicate dark places; in the *Samson Agonistes* (86–89):

> The Sun to me is dark
> And silent as the Moon,
> When she deserts the night
> Hid in her vacant interlunar cave.

Cf. E. M. W. Tillyard, *The Miltonic Setting*, 101.

performs innumerable feats and Don Quixote is beaten and derided, but Don Quixote's worth is felt more deeply. This leads us to an aesthetic problem not posed heretofore: Can an author create characters that are superior to himself? I would reply that he cannot, and my negation would apply to the intellectual as well as the moral levels. I believe that creatures who are more lucid or more noble than our best moments will not issue from us. On that opinion I base my conviction of the pre-eminence of Shaw. The problems about labor unions and municipalities of his early works will cease to be interesting, or else have already done so; the jokes of the Pleasant Plays bid fair to being, some day, no less awkward than Shakespeare's (humor, I suspect, is an oral genre, a sudden spark in conversation, not a written thing); the ideas expressed by the prologues and the eloquent tirades will be sought in Schopenhauer and in Samuel Butler;[2] but Lavinia, Blanco Posnet, Keegan, Shotover, Richard Dudgeon, and, above all, Julius Caesar, surpass any character imagined by the art of our time. To think of Monsieur Teste or the histrionic Zarathustra of Nietzsche alongside them is to apprehend, with surprise or even astonishment, the primacy of Shaw. In 1911 Albert Soergel was able to write, repeating a commonplace of the time, "Bernard Shaw is an annihilator of the heroic concept, a killer of heroes" (*Dichtung und Dichter der Zeit*, 214); he did not understand that the heroic was completely independent from the romantic and was embodied in Captain Bluntschli of *Arms and the Man*, not in Sergius Saranoff.

The biography of Bernard Shaw by Frank Harris contains an admirable letter written by Shaw, in which he says: "I understand everything and everyone, and am nobody and nothing" (p. 228). From that nothingness (so comparable to the nothingness of God before He created the world, so comparable to the primordial divinity that another Irishman, Johannes Scotus Erigena, called *Nihil*), Bernard Shaw educed almost innumerable persons, or dramatis personae: the

---

[2] Also in Swedenborg. In *Man and Superman* we read that Hell is not a penal establishment but a state that dead sinners choose, because they feel an affinity with it, just as the good choose Heaven. Swedenborg's treatise *De Coelo et Inferno*, published in 1758, expresses the same doctrine.

most ephemeral, I suspect, is G. B. S., who represented him to the public and who supplied such a wealth of easy witticisms for newspaper columns.

Shaw's basic subjects are philosophy and ethics: it is natural and inevitable that he is not esteemed in Argentina, or that he is remembered in that country only for a few epigrams. The Argentine feels that the universe is nothing but a manifestation of chance, the fortuitous combination of atoms conceived by Democritus; philosophy does not interest him. Nor does ethics: for him, social problems are nothing but a conflict of individuals or classes or nations, in which everything is licit—except ridicule or defeat.

Man's character and its variations constitute the essential theme of the novel of our time; the lyric is the complacent magnification of amorous fortunes or misfortunes; the philosophies of Heidegger or Jaspers transform each one of us into the interesting interlocutor of a secret and continuous dialogue with nothingness or with divinity; these disciplines, which may be formally admirable, foster the illusion of the self that Vedanta condemns as a capital error. They may play at desperation and anguish, but at bottom they flatter the vanity; in that sense, they are immoral. Shaw's work, on the other hand, leaves an aftertaste of liberation. The taste of the doctrines of Zeno's Porch and the taste of the sagas.

Buenos Aires, 1951

166

The Modesty of History

On September 20, 1792, Johann Wolfgang von Goethe (who had accompanied the Duke of Weimar on a military expedition to Paris) saw the finest army of Europe inexplicably repulsed at Valmy by some French militiamen, and said to his disconcerted friends: "In this place and on this day, a new epoch in the history of the world is beginning, and we shall be able to say that we have been present at its origin." Since that time historic days have been numerous, and one of the tasks of governments (especially in Italy, Germany, and Russia) has been to fabricate them or to simulate them with an abundance of preconditioning propaganda followed by relentless publicity. Such days, which reveal the influence of Cecil B. De Mille, are related less to history than to journalism. I have suspected that history, real history, is more modest and that its essential dates may be, for a long time, secret. A Chinese prose writer has observed that the unicorn, because of its own anomaly, will pass unnoticed. Our eyes see what they are accustomed to seeing. Tacitus did not perceive the Crucifixion, although his book recorded it.

Those thoughts came to me after a phrase happened to catch my eye as I leafed through a history of Greek literature. The phrase aroused my interest because of its enigmatic quality: "He brought in a second actor." I stopped; I found that the subject of that mysterious action was Aeschylus and that, as we read in the fourth chapter of

167

Aristotle's *Poetics*, he "raised the number of actors from one to two." It is well known that the drama was an offshoot of the religion of Dionysus. Originally, a single actor, the *hypokritēs*, elevated by the cothurnus, dressed in black or purple and with his face enlarged by a mask, shared the scene with the twelve individuals of the chorus. The drama was one of the ceremonies of the worship and, like all ritual, was in danger of remaining invariable. Aeschylus' innovation could have occurred on but one day, five hundred years before the Christian era; the Athenians saw with amazement and perhaps with shock (Victor Hugo thought the latter) the unannounced appearance of a second actor. On that remote spring day, in that honey-colored theatre, what did they think, what did they feel exactly? Perhaps neither amazement nor shock; perhaps only a beginning of surprise. In the *Tusculanae* it is stated that Aeschylus joined the Pythagorean order, but we shall never know if he had a prefiguring, even an imperfect one, of the importance of that passage from one to two, from unity to plurality and thus to infinity. With the second actor came the dialogue and the indefinite possibilities of the reaction of some characters on others. A prophetic spectator would have seen that multitudes of future appearances accompanied him: Hamlet and Faust and Segismundo and Macbeth and Peer Gynt and others our eyes cannot yet discern.

I found another historic day in the course of my reading. It occurred in Iceland in the thirteenth century; let us say in 1225. For the instruction of future generations, the historian and polygrapher Snorri Sturlason, at his estate in Borgarfjord, wrote about the last exploit of the famous King Harald Sigurdarson, also called the Implacable (Hardrada), who fought in Byzantium, Italy, and Africa. Tostig, the brother of the Saxon King of England, Harold Godwinson, coveted the power and had obtained the help of Harald Sigurdarson. With an army of Norsemen, they landed on the eastern shore and subdued the castle of Jorvik (York). South of Jorvik they were confronted by the Saxon army. Snorri's text continues:

Twenty horsemen joined the ranks of the invader; the men and also the horses were covered with mail. One of the horsemen shouted, "Is Earl Tostig here?"

168

"I do not deny that I am here," said the Earl.

"If you are really Tostig," said the horseman, "I come to tell you that your brother offers you his pardon and a third part of the kingdom."

"If I accept," said Tostig, "what will the King give to Harald Sigurdarson?"

"He has not forgotten him," replied the horseman. "He will give him six feet of English sod and since he is so tall, one more."

"Then," said Tostig, "tell your king we shall fight to the death."

The horsemen galloped away. Harald Sigurdarson asked pensively, "Who was that man who spoke so well?"

"Harold Godwinson."

Other chapters tell that before the sun set that day the Norse army was defeated. Harald Sigurdarson died in the battle and so did the Earl (*Heimskringla*, X, 92).

There is a flavor that our time (perhaps surfeited by the clumsy imitations of professional patriots) does not usually perceive without some suspicion: the fundamental flavor of the heroic. People assure me that the *Poema del Cid* has that flavor; I have found it, unmistakably, in verses of the *Aeneid* ("My son, from me learn valor and true constancy; from others, success"), in the Anglo-Saxon ballad of Maldon ("My people will pay the tribute with lances and with old swords"), in the *Chanson de Roland*, in Victor Hugo, in Whitman, and in Faulkner ("the single sprig of it ⌈verbena⌉ . . . filling the room, the dusk, the evening with that odor which she said you could smell alone above the smell of horses"), in Housman's "Epitaph on an Army of Mercenaries," and in the "six feet of English sod" of the *Heimskringla*. Behind the apparent simplicity of the historian there is a delicate psychological game. Harold pretends not to recognize his brother, so that the latter, in turn, will perceive that he must not recognize him either; Tostig does not betray him, nor will he betray his ally; Harold, willing to pardon his brother but not to tolerate the meddling of the Norse King, proceeds in a very comprehensible manner. I shall say nothing of the verbal skill of his reply: to give a third of the kingdom, to give six feet of sod.[1]

Only one thing is more admirable than the admirable reply of the

---

[1] Carlyle (*Early Kings of Norway*, XI) spoils this economy with an unfortunate addition. To "the six feet of English sod" he adds "for a grave."

Saxon king: that an Icelander, a man of the lineage of the vanquished, has perpetuated the reply. It is as if a Carthaginian had bequeathed to us the memory of the exploit of Regulus. Saxo Grammaticus wrote with justification in his *Gesta Danorum*: "The men of Thule [Iceland] are very fond of learning and of recording the history of all peoples and they are equally pleased to reveal the excellences of others or of themselves."

Not the day when the Saxon said the words, but the day when an enemy perpetuated them, was the historic date. A date that is a prophecy of something still in the future: the day when races and nations will be cast into oblivion, and the solidarity of all mankind will be established. The offer owes its virtue to the concept of a fatherland. By relating it, Snorri surmounts and transcends that concept.

I recall another tribute to an enemy in one of the last chapters of Lawrence's *Seven Pillars of Wisdom*. The author praises the valor of a German detachment and writes that for the first time in the campaign he was proud of the men who had killed his brothers. And he adds: "They were glorious."

Buenos Aires, 1952

170

New Refutation of Time

Vor mir war keine Zeit, nach mir wird keine seyn,
Mit mir gebiert sie sich, mit mir geht sie auch ein.
Daniel von Czepko: *Sexcenta monodisticha*
sapientum (1655) III, ii

PROLOGUE

Published at the middle of the eighteenth century, this refutation (or its name) would endure in the bibliographies of Hume
and perhaps would have been mentioned by Huxley or Kemp Smith.
Published in 1947—after Bergson—it is the anachronous *reductio ad*
absurdum of an obsolete system or, what is worse, the feeble machina-
tion of an Argentine adrift on the sea of metaphysics. Both conjectures are verisimilar and perhaps true; to correct them I cannot
promise a startling conclusion in exchange for my rudimentary dialectic. The thesis I shall expound is as ancient as Zeno's arrow or the
chariot of the Greek king in the *Milinda Pañha*; whatever novelty it
possesses consists in the application of Berkeley's classic instrument
to that end. Berkeley and his successor, David Hume, abound in paragraphs that contradict or exclude my thesis; nevertheless, I believe
I have deduced the inevitable consequence of their doctrine.

The first article (*A*) is from 1944 and appeared in Number 115 of *Sur*; the second article (*B*), from 1946, is a revision of the first. I deliberately did not combine the two into one article, because I knew that the reading of two similar texts could facilitate the understanding of an indocile subject.

A word about the title. I am not unaware that it is an example of the monster which logicians have called *contradictio in adjecto*, because to say that a refutation of time is new (or old) is to attribute to it a predicate of a temporal nature, which restores the notion that the subject attempts to destroy. But I shall let it stand, so that this very subtle joke may prove that I do not exaggerate the importance of these word games. Apart from that, our language is so saturated and animated with time that it is very possible that not one line in this book does not somehow demand or invoke it.

I dedicate these studies to my ancestor, Juan Crisóstomo Lafinur (1797–1824), who has left Argentine letters some memorable poetry, and who tried to reform the teaching of philosophy by purifying it from theological shadows and exposing the principles of Locke and Condillac. He died in exile; like all men, he was born at the wrong time.

J. L. B.

Buenos Aires, December 23, 1946

A

I

In the course of a life dedicated to literature and, occasionally, to metaphysical perplexity, I have perceived or sensed a refutation of time, which I myself disbelieve, but which comes to visit me at night and in the weary dawns with the illusory force of an axiom. That refutation is in all my books in one way or another: there is a prefiguring of it in the poems "Inscripción en cualquier sepulcro" and "El truco," from my volume of poetry *Fervor de Buenos Aires* (1923); it is declared in two articles in my book *Inquisiciones* (1925), on page 46 of *Evaristo Carriego* (1930), in the story "Sentirse en muerte" from my *Historia de la eternidad* (1936), and in the note on page 24 of my *El jardín de senderos que se bifurcan* (1942).

None of the texts I have enumerated satisfies me, not even "Sentirse en muerte," which is less demonstrative and reasoned than divinatory and pathetic. I shall try to consolidate them all with this article.

Two arguments led me to this refutation: Berkeley's idealism and Leibnitz's principle of indiscernibles.

Berkeley (*The Principles of Human Knowledge*, 3) observed:

That neither our thoughts, nor passions, nor ideas formed by the imagination, exist without the mind, is what everybody will allow.—And to me it is no less evident that the various *Sensations*, or *ideas imprinted on the sense*, however blended or combined together (that is, whatever *objects* they compose), cannot exist otherwise than in a mind perceiving them — ... The table I write on I say exists, that is, I see and feel it; and if I were out of my study I should say it existed—meaning thereby that if I was in my study I might perceive it, or that some other spirit actually does perceive it. ... For as to what is said of the absolute existence of unthinking things without any relation to their being perceived, that is to me perfectly unintelligible. Their *esse* is *percipi*, nor is it possible they should have any existence out of the minds or thinking things which perceive them.

Foreseeing objections, he added in Paragraph 23:

But, say you, surely there is nothing easier than for me to imagine trees, for instance, in a park, or books existing in a closet, and nobody by to perceive them. I answer, you may so, there is no difficulty in it; but what is all this, I beseech you, more than framing in *your* mind certain ideas which you call books and trees, and at the same time omitting to frame the idea of any one that may perceive them? But do not you yourself perceive or think of them all the while? This therefore is nothing to the purpose: it only shews you have the power of imagining or forming ideas in your mind; but it does not shew that you can conceive it possible the objects of your thought may exist without the mind.

In Paragraph 6, he had already stated:

Some truths there are so near and obvious to the mind that a man need only open his eyes to see them. Such I take this important one to be, viz., that all the choir of heaven and furniture of the earth, in a word all those bodies which compose the mighty frame of the world, have not any subsistence without a mind—that their *being* is *to be perceived or known*; that consequently so long as they are not actually perceived by me, or do

173

not exist in my mind or that of any other created spirit, they must either have no existence at all, or else subsist in the mind of some Eternal Spirit—.

That, in the words of its inventor, is the idealist doctrine. Understanding it is easy; the difficult thing is to think within its limits. Schopenhauer himself, when he explains it, commits culpable negligences. In the first lines of the first book of his *Welt als Wille und Vorstellung*—in the year 1819—he makes the following statement, which entitles him to the imperishable bewilderment of all men: "The world is my representation. The man who confesses this truth is well aware that he does not know a sun or an earth, but only some eyes that see a sun and a hand that feels the contact of an earth." That is to say, for the idealist Schopenhauer man's eyes and hand are less illusory or apparential than the earth and the sun. In 1844 he publishes a supplementary volume. In the first chapter he rediscovers and exaggerates the old error: he defines the universe as a cerebral phenomenon and distinguishes "the world in the head" from "the world outside of the head." But in 1713 Berkeley had made Philonous say: "The brain therefore you speak of, being a sensible thing, exists only in the mind. Now, I would fain know whether you think it reasonable to suppose, that one idea or thing existing in the mind, occasions all other ideas. And if you think so, pray how do you account for the origin of that primary idea or brain itself?"

The dualism or cerebralism of Schopenhauer can be opposed effectively to the monism of Spiller. The latter (*The Mind of Man*, 1902, Chapter VIII) argues that the retina and the cutaneous surface invoked to explain the visual and the tactile are, in turn, two tactile and visual systems; and that the room we see (the "objective") is no larger than the imagined one (the "cerebral") and does not contain it, since they are two independent visual systems. Berkeley (*The Principles of Human Knowledge*, pp. 10 and 116) also denied the primary qualities—the solidity and the extension of things—and absolute space.

Berkeley affirmed the continuous existence of objects, since even if some individual did not perceive them, God perceived them. More logically, Hume denied it (*A Treatise of Human Nature*, I, 4, 2).

Berkeley affirmed personal identity, because "I myself am not my ideas, but somewhat else, a thinking, active principle" (*Dialogues*, 3). Hume, the skeptic, refuted it and made each man "a bundle or collection of different perceptions, which succeed each other with an inconceivable rapidity" (*A Treatise*, I, 4, 6). They both affirm time: for Berkeley it is "the succession of ideas in my mind, which flows uniformly and is participated by all beings" (*The Principles of Human Knowledge*, 98); for Hume time "must be composed of indivisible moments" (*A Treatise*, I, 2, 2).

I have amassed some quotations from the apologists of idealism, I have offered their canonical passages, I have been iterative and explicit, I have censured Schopenhauer (not without ingratitude), to help my reader penetrate that unstable mental world. A world of evanescent impressions; a world without matter or spirit, neither objective nor subjective; a world without the ideal architecture of space; a world made of time, of the absolute uniform time of the *Principia*; an indefatigable labyrinth, a chaos, a dream—the almost complete disintegration to which David Hume came.

Once the idealist argument is admitted, I believe that it is possible —perhaps inevitable—to go further. For Hume it is not licit to speak of the shape of the moon or of its color; the shape and the color *are* the moon; nor can one speak of the perceptions of the mind, since the mind is nothing more than a series of perceptions. The Cartesian "I think, therefore I am" is invalidated. To say "I think" is to postulate the ego; it is a *petitio principii*. In the eighteenth century Lichtenberg proposed that instead of "I think," we should say impersonally "it thinks," as we say "it thunders" or "it lightens." I repeat: there is not a secret ego behind faces that governs actions and receives impressions; we are only the series of those imaginary actions and those errant impressions. The series? If we deny spirit and matter, which are continuities, and if we deny space also, I do not know what right we have to the continuity that is time.

Imagine any present. On a Mississippi night Huckleberry Finn awakens. The raft, lost in the partial darkness, is floating down the river. Perhaps the weather is cool. Huckleberry Finn recognizes the quiet relentless sound of the water; he opens his eyes lazily. He sees a vague number of stars, he sees an indistinct streak of trees; then he sinks into an immemorial sleep that envelops him like murky water.[1] The metaphysics of idealism declare that it is risky and futile to add a material substance (the object) and a spiritual substance (the subject) to those perceptions. I maintain that it is no less illogical to think that they are terms of a series whose beginning is as inconceivable as its end. To add to the river and the shore perceived by Huck the notion of another substantive river and another shore, to add another perception to that immediate network of perceptions is, for idealism, unjustifiable. For me, it is no less unjustifiable to add chronological precision: the fact, for example, that the event occurred on June 7, 1849, between 4:10 and 4:11 A.M. Or in other words: I deny, with the arguments of idealism, the vast temporal series that idealism admits. Hume has denied the existence of absolute space, in which each thing has its place; I deny the existence of one time, in which all events are linked together. To deny coexistence is no less difficult than to deny succession.

I deny the successive, in a large number of cases; I deny the contemporaneous also, in a large number of cases. The lover who thinks, "While I was so happy, thinking of my loved one's fidelity, she was deceiving me," deceives himself: if each state we live is absolute, that happiness was not contemporaneous with that deceit; the discovery of that deceit is one more state, incapable of modifying the "previous" ones, but not the remembrance of them. The misfortune of today is no more real than past happiness. I shall give a more concrete example. At the beginning of August, 1824, Captain Isidoro Suárez, leading a squadron of Peruvian Hussars, achieved the victory of Junín; at the beginning of August, 1824, De Quincey published a diatribe against *Wilhelm Meisters Lehrjahre*. Those events were not contemporaneous (they are now), for the two men died, Suárez in the city of Montevideo, De Quincey in Edinburgh, each without knowing of the other. Every instant is autonomous. Neither revenge nor pardon nor prisons nor even oblivion can modify the invulnerable past. No less vain to me are hope and fear, which always relate to future events: that is, to events that will not happen to us, who are the

[1] For the facility of the reader, I have selected an instant between two dreams, a literary instant, not a historical one. If anyone suspects a fallacy, he can insert another example; from his own life, if he wishes.

minutiae of the present. I am told that the present, the "specious present" of the psychologists, lasts between several seconds and a tiny fraction of a second; that is how long the history of the universe lasts. Or rather, there is no such history, as there is no life of a man, nor even one of his nights; each moment we live exists, not its imaginary aggregate. The universe, the sum of all the events, is a collection that is no less ideal than that of all the horses Shakespeare dreamed— one, many, none?—between 1592 and 1594. I might add that if time is a mental process, how can it be shared by thousands, or even two different men?

Interrupted and burdened by examples, the argument of the foregoing paragraphs may seem intricate. I shall try a more direct method. Let us consider a life in which repetitions are abundant; mine, for example. I never pass Recoleta cemetery without remembering that my father, my grandparents, and my great-grandparents are buried there, as I shall be; then I remember that I have already remembered that, many times before. I cannot walk down my neighborhood streets in the solitude of night without thinking that night is pleasing to us because, like memory, it erases idle details. I cannot mourn the loss of a love or a friendship without reflecting that one can lose only what one has never really had. Each time I come to a certain place in the South, I think of you, Helen; each time the air brings me a scent of eucalyptus, I think of Adrogué, in my childhood; each time I remember Fragment 91 of Heraclitus: "You will not go down twice to the same river," I admire his dialectic skill, because the facility with which we accept the first meaning ("The river is different") clandestinely imposes the second one ("I am different") and gives us the illusion of having invented it. Each time I hear a Germanophile vituperating Yiddish, I pause and think that Yiddish is, after all, a German dialect, barely maculated by the language of the Holy Spirit. Those tautologies (and others I shall not disclose) are my whole life. Naturally, they are repeated without precision; there are differences of emphasis, temperature, light, general physiological state. But I suspect that the number of circumstantial variations is not infinite: we can postulate, in the mind of an individual (or of two individuals who do not know each other, but on whom the same process is acting), two identical moments. Having postulated that identity, we must ask: Are those identical moments the same? Is *a single repeated term* enough to disrupt and confound the series of time? Are the enthusiasts who devote a lifetime to a line by Shakespeare not literally Shakespeare?

I am still not certain of the ethics of the system I have outlined. I do not know whether it exists. The fifth paragraph of Chapter Four in the "Sanhedrin" of the Mishnah declares that, for the Justice of God, he who kills a single man destroys the world; if there is no plurality, he who annihilated all men would be no more guilty than the primitive and solitary Cain, which is orthodox, nor more universal in his destruction, which can be magic. I believe that is true. The tumultuous general catastrophes—fires, wars, epidemics—are but a single sorrow, illusorily multiplied in many mirrors. That is Bernard Shaw's judgment when he states (*Guide to Socialism*, 86) that what one person can suffer is the maximum that can be suffered on earth. If one person dies of inanition, he will suffer all the inanition that has been or will be. If ten thousand other persons die with him, he will not be ten thousand times hungrier nor will he suffer ten thousand times longer. There is no point in being overwhelmed by the appalling total of human suffering; such a total does not exist. Neither poverty nor pain is accumulable. Compare also *The Problem of Pain* (VII) by C. S. Lewis.

Lucretius (*De rerum natura*, I, 830) attributes to Anaxagoras the doctrine that gold consists of particles of gold; fire, of sparks; bone, of imperceptible little bones. Josiah Royce, perhaps influenced by St. Augustine, believes that time consists of time and that "Every *now* within which something happens is therefore *also* a succession" (*The World and the Individual*, II, 139). That proposition is compatible with my own.

II

All language is of a successive nature; it is not an effective tool for reasoning the eternal, the intemporal. Those who were displeased with the foregoing argumentation might prefer this piece from 1928 which is part of the story "Sentirse en muerte," mentioned earlier in this article:

And here I should like to record an experience I had several nights ago: too evanescent and ecstatic a trifle to be called an adventure; too unreasonable and sentimental to be a thought. There is a scene and a word: a word I had said before but never lived with complete dedication until that night. I shall relate it now, with the accidents of time and place that brought about its revelation.

I remember it this way. I had spent the afternoon in Barracas, a place I rarely visited, a place whose very distance from the scene of my later wanderings gave an aura of strangeness to that day. As I had nothing to do in the evening and the weather was fair, I went out after dinner to walk and remember. I did not wish to have a set destination. I followed a random course, as much as possible; I accepted, with no conscious prejudice other than avoiding the avenues or wide streets, the most obscure invitations of chance. But a kind of familiar gravitation drew me toward certain sections I shall always remember, for they arouse in me a kind of reverence. I am not speaking of the precise environment of my childhood, my own neighborhood, but of the still mysterious fringe area beyond it, which I have possessed completely in words and but little in reality, an area that is familiar and mythological at the same time. The opposite of the known—its wrong side, so to speak—are those streets to me, almost as completely hidden as the buried foundation of our house or our invisible skeleton.

The walk brought me to a corner. I breathed the night, feeling the peaceful respite from thought. The sight that greeted my eyes, uncomplicated to be sure, seemed simplified by my fatigue. Its very typicality made it unreal. The street was lined with low houses, and, although the first impression was poverty, the second was surely happiness. The street was very poor and very pretty. None of the houses stood out from the rest; the fig tree cast a shadow; the doors—higher than the elongated lines of the walls—seemed to be made of the same infinite substance as the night. The footpath ran along steeply above the street, which was of elemental clay, clay of a still unconquered America. To the rear the alley was already the pampa, descending toward the Maldonado. On the muddy and chaotic ground a rose-colored adobe wall seemed not to harbor moonglow but to shed a light of its own. I suspect that there can be no better way of denoting tenderness than by means of that rose color.

I stood there looking at that simplicity. I thought, no doubt aloud, "This is the same as it was thirty years ago." I guessed at the date: a recent time in other countries, but already remote in this changing part of the world. Perhaps a bird was singing and I felt for him a small, bird-sized affection. What stands out most clearly: in the already vertiginous silence the only noise was the intemporal sound of the crickets. The easy thought, "I am in the eighteen hundreds" ceased to be a few careless words and deepened into reality. I felt dead—that I was an abstract perceiver of the world; I felt an undefined fear imbued with knowledge, the supreme clarity of metaphysics. No, I did not believe I had traveled across the presumptive waters of Time; rather I suspected I was the possessor of the reticent or absent meaning of the inconceivable word *eternity*. Only later was I able to define that imagining.

And now I shall write it like this: that pure representation of homogeneous facts—clear night, limpid wall, rural scent of honeysuckle, elemental clay—is not merely identical to the scene on that corner so many years ago; it is, without similarities or repetitions, the same. If we can perceive that identity, time is a delusion: the indifference and inseparability of one moment of time's apparent yesterday and another of its apparent today are enough to disintegrate it.

It is evident that the number of these human moments is not infinite. The basic ones are still more impersonal—moments of physical suffering and physical joy, of the approach of sleep, of the hearing of a single piece of music, of much intensity or much dejection. This is the conclusion I derive: life is too poor not to be immortal. But we do not even possess the certainty of our poverty, since time, easily refutable in the area of the senses, is not so easily refutable in the intellectual sphere, from whose essence the concept of succession seems inseparable. So then, let my intimation of an idea remain as an emotional anecdote. The real moment of ecstasy and the possible insinuation of eternity which that night so generously bestowed on me will be crystalized in the avowed irresolution of these pages.

B

Of the many doctrines recorded by the history of philosophy, idealism is perhaps the most ancient and the most widely divulged. The observation is Carlyle's (*Novalis*, 1829). Without any hope of completing the infinite census, I should like to add to the philosophers he mentioned the Platonists, for whom prototypes are the only reality (Norris, Judah Abrabanel, Gemistus, Plotinus); the theologians, for whom everything that is not the divinity is contingent (Malebranche, Johannes Eckhart); the monists, who make of the universe a vain

180

adjective of the Absolute (Bradley, Hegel, Parmenides). Idealism is as old as metaphysical inquietude. Its most clever apologist, George Berkeley, flourished in the eighteenth century. Contrary to Schopenhauer's statement (*Welt als Wille und Vorstellung*, II, I), Berkeley's merit could not have consisted in the intuitive perception of that doctrine, but in the arguments he conceived to reason it. Berkeley utilized those arguments against the notion of matter; Hume applied them to consciousness. My purpose is to apply them to time. But first I shall summarize briefly the various stages of that dialectic.

Berkeley denied matter. That does not mean, it should be understood, that he denied colors, odors, flavors, sounds, and contacts. What he denied was that, outside of those perceptions or components of the external world, there was an invisible, intangible something called matter. He denied that there were pains that no one feels, colors that no one sees, forms that no one touches. He reasoned that to add matter to perceptions is to add to the world an inconceivable superfluous world. He believed in the apparential world fabricated by the senses, but he considered that the material world (Toland's, say) was an illusory duplication. He observed (*The Principles of Human Knowledge*, 3):

That neither our thoughts, nor passions, nor ideas formed by the imagination, exist without the mind, is what everybody will allow.—And to me it is no less evident that the various *Sensations*, or *ideas imprinted on the sense*, however blended or combined together (that is, whatever *objects* they compose), cannot exist otherwise than in a mind perceiving them,— . . . The table I write on I say exists, that is, I see and feel it; and if I were out of my study I should say it existed—meaning thereby that if I was in my study I might perceive it, or that some other spirit actually does perceive it. . . . For as to what is said of the absolute existence of unthinking things without any relation to their being perceived, that is to me perfectly unintelligible. Their *esse* is *percipi*, nor is it possible they should have any existence out of the minds or thinking things which perceive them.

Foreseeing objections, he added in Paragraph 23:

But, say you, surely there is nothing easier than for me to imagine trees, for instance, in a park, or books existing in a closet, and nobody by

181

to perceive them. I answer, you may so, there is no difficulty in it; but what is all this, I beseech you, more than framing in *your* mind certain ideas which you call books and trees, and at the same time omitting to frame the idea of any one that may perceive them? But do not you yourself perceive or think of them all the while? This therefore is nothing to the purpose; it only shews you have the power of imagining or forming ideas in your mind; but it does not shew that you can conceive it possible the objects of your thought may exist without the mind.

In Paragraph 6 he had already stated:

Some truths there are so near and obvious to the mind that a man need only open his eyes to see them. Such I take this important one to be, viz., that all the choir of heaven and furniture of the earth, in a word all those bodies which compose the mighty frame of the world, have not any subsistence without a mind—that their *being* is *to be perceived or known;* that consequently so long as they are not actually perceived by me, or do not exist in my mind or that of any other created spirit, they must either have no existence at all, or else subsist in the mind of some Eternal Spirit—.

(Berkeley's God is a ubiquitous spectator whose purpose is to give coherence to the world.)

The doctrine I have just expounded has been misinterpreted. Herbert Spencer believes he refutes it (*Principles of Psychology,* VIII, 6) by reasoning that if there is nothing but consciousness, then it must be infinite in time and space. It is true that consciousness is infinite in time if we understand that all time is time perceived by someone, and false if we infer that that time must, necessarily, span an infinite number of centuries. That consciousness must be infinite in space is illicit, since Berkeley (*The Principles of Human Knowledge,* 116; *Siris,* 266) repeatedly denied absolute space. Even more indecipherable is the error Schopenhauer makes (*Welt als Wille und Vorstellung,* II, I) when he teaches that for the idealists the world is a cerebral phenomenon. However, Berkeley had written (*Dialogues between Hylas and Philonous,* II): "The brain . . . being a sensible thing, exists only in the mind. Now, I would fain know whether you think it reasonable to suppose, that one idea or thing existing in the mind, occasions all other ideas. And if you think so, pray how do you account for the origin of that primary idea or brain itself?" The

182

brain, in fact, is no less a part of the external world than the constellation Centaurus.

Berkeley denied that there was an object behind sense impressions. David Hume denied that there was a subject behind the perception of changes. Berkeley denied matter; Hume denied the spirit. Berkeley did not wish us to add the metaphysical notion of matter to the succession of impressions, while Hume did not wish us to add the metaphysical notion of a self to the succession of mental states. This amplification of Berkeley's arguments is so logical that Berkeley had already foreseen it, as Alexander Campbell Fraser points out, and had even tried to confute it by means of the Cartesian *ergo sum*. Hylas, foreshadowing David Hume, had said in the third and last of the *Dialogues*: " . . . in consequence of your own principles, it should follow that you are only a system of floating ideas, without any substance to support them. . . . And as there is no more meaning in spiritual substance than in material substance, the one is to be exploded as well as the other." Hume corroborates this:

. . . I may venture to affirm of the rest of mankind, that they are nothing but a bundle or collection of different perceptions, which succeed each other with an inconceivable rapidity . . . The mind is a kind of theatre, where several perceptions successively make their appearance; pass, re-pass, glide away, and mingle in an infinite variety of postures and situations. . . . The comparison of the theatre must not mislead us. They are the successive perceptions only, that constitute the mind; nor have we the most distant notion of the place where these scenes are represented, or of the materials of which it is composed. (*A Treatise of Human Nature*, I, 4, 6)

Having admitted the idealist argument, I believe it is possible—perhaps inevitable—to go further. For Berkeley, time is "the succession of ideas . . . which flows uniformly and is participated by all beings" (*The Principles of Human Knowledge*, 98); for Hume it is "composed of indivisible moments" (*A Treatise of Human Nature*, I, 2, 2). Nevertheless, having denied matter and spirit, which are continuities, and having denied space also, I do not know with what right we shall retain the continuity that is time. Outside of each perception (actual or conjectural) matter does not exist; outside of each mental state the spirit does not exist; nor will time exist outside of each present instant. Let us select a moment of the greatest simplicity, that of the dream of Chuang Tzu (Herbert Allen Giles: *Chuang Tzu,* 1889). Around twenty-four hundred years ago Chuang Tzu dreamed that he was a butterfly and when he awakened he did not know if he was a man who had dreamed he was a butterfly, or a butterfly dreaming it was a man. Let us not consider the awakening; let us consider the moment of the dream; or one of the moments. "I dreamed that I was a butterfly flying through the air and that I knew nothing of Chuang Tzu," says the ancient text. We shall never know if Chuang Tzu saw a garden over which he seemed to be flying, or a moving yellow triangle, which was undoubtedly he himself, but we know that the image was subjective, although it was supplied by the memory. The doctrine of psychophysical parallelism will avow that this image must have been caused by some change in the dreamer's nervous system; according to Berkeley, at that moment neither Chuang Tzu's body nor the black bedroom in which he dreamed existed, except as a perception in the divine mind. Hume simplifies it even more: at that moment Chuang Tzu's spirit did not exist; only the colors of the dream and the certainty of being a butterfly existed. It existed as a momentary term of the "bundle or collection of different perceptions" which was, some four centuries before Christ, the mind of Chuang Tzu; they existed as term n of an infinite temporal series, between $n - 1$ and $n + 1$. There is no other reality for idealism than that of the mental processes; to add to the butterfly that is perceived an objective butterfly seems to be a vain duplication; to add an ego to the processes seems no less excessive. It acknowledges that there was a dreaming, a perceiving, but not a dreamer or even a dream; and that to speak of objects and of subjects is to gravitate toward an impure mythology. Now then, if each psychic state is self-sufficient, if to connect it to a circumstance or to an ego is an illicit and vain addition, what right have we to impose on it, later, a place in time? Chuang Tzu dreamed that he was a butterfly and during that dream he was not Chuang Tzu—he was a butterfly. How, having abolished space and the ego, shall we connect those instants to the instants of awakening and to the feudal age of Chinese history? That does not mean that we shall never know, even approximately, the date of the dream; it means that the chronological determination of an event, of

184

any event on earth, is alien and exterior to the event. In China, Chuang Tzu's dream is proverbial; imagine that one of its almost infinite readers dreams he is a butterfly and then that he is Chuang Tzu. Imagine that, by a not impossible chance, this dream is an exact repetition of the master's dream. Having postulated that identity, we must ask: Those instants that coincide—are they not the same? Is not *one single repeated term* enough to disrupt and confound the history of the world, to tell us that there is no such history?

To deny time is really two denials: the denial of the succession of the terms of a series, the denial of the synchronism of the terms of two series. In fact, if each term is absolute, its relations are reduced to the consciousness that those relations exist. One state precedes another if it is known to be anterior to it; State *G* is contemporaneous with State *H* if it is known to be contemporaneous with it. Contrary to Schopenhauer's declaration[2] in his table of fundamental truths (*Welt als Wille und Vorstellung*, II, 4), each fraction of time does not fill all space simultaneously, time is not ubiquitous. (Naturally, at this stage of the argument, space no longer exists.)

Meinong, in his theory of apprehension, admits the apprehension of imaginary objects: the fourth dimension, say, or the sensible statue of Condillac, or the hypothetical animal of Lotze, or the square root of—*I*. If the reasons I have indicated are valid, then matter, the ego, the external world, universal history, our lives also belong to that nebulous orb.

Furthermore, the phrase *negation of time* is ambiguous. It can mean the eternity of Plato or Boethius and also the dilemmas of Sextus Empiricus. The latter (*Adversus mathematicos*, XI, 197) denies the past, which already was, and the future, which has not yet been, and argues that the present is divisible or indivisible. It is not indivisible, because in that case it would have no beginning that would connect it to the past nor end that would connect it to the future, nor even a middle, because a thing that has no beginning and end cannot have a middle; neither is it divisible, because in that case it would consist of a part that was and of another part that is not.

---

[2] And previously by Newton, who affirmed: "Each particle of space is eternal, each indivisible moment of duration is everywhere" (*Principia*, III, 42).

Ergo, the present does not exist, and since the past and the future do not exist either, time does not exist. F. H. Bradley rediscovers and improves that perplexity. He observes (*Appearance and Reality*, IV) that if the now is divisible into other nows it is no less complicated than time, and, if it is indivisible, time is a mere relation between intemporal things. As you see, those reasonings deny the parts in order to deny the whole; I reject the whole to exalt each one of the parts. By the dialectic of Berkeley and Hume I have arrived at Schopenhauer's statement:

The form of the appearance of the will is only the present, not the past or the future; the latter do not exist except in the concept and by the linking of the consciousness, submitted to the principle of reason. No one has lived in the past, no one will live in the future; the present is the form of all life, it is a possession that no misfortune can take away . . . Time is like an infinitely rotating circle: the descending arc is the past, the ascending one is the future; above, there is an indivisible point that touches the tangent and is the now. Motionless like the tangent, that extensionless point marks the contact of the object, whose form is time, with the subject, which is formless, because it does not belong to the knowable and is a preliminary condition of knowledge. (*Welt als Wille und Vorstellung*, I, 54)

A Buddhist tract from the fifth century, the *Visuddhimagga* (*Way of Purity*), illustrates the same doctrine with the same figure: "Strictly speaking, the life of a being has the duration of an idea. As a carriage wheel touches the ground in only one place when it turns, life lasts as long as a single idea" (Radhakrishnan: *Indian Philosophy*, I, 373). Other Buddhist texts say that the world is annihilated and resurges again 6,500,000,000 times a day and that every man is an illusion, vertiginously made of a series of momentary and lone men. "The man of a past moment," says the *Way of Purity*, "has lived, but he does not live nor will he live; the man of a future moment will live, but he has not lived nor does he live; the man of the present moment lives, but he has not lived nor will he live" (*Indian Philosophy*, I, 407). We can compare this with the words of Plutarch (*De E apud Delphos*, 18): "The man of yesterday has died in the man of today, the man of today dies in the man of tomorrow."

And yet, and yet—To deny temporal succession, to deny the ego, to deny the astronomical universe, are apparent desperations and secret assuagements. Our destiny (unlike the hell of Swedenborg and the hell of Tibetan mythology) is not horrible because of its unreality; it is horrible because it is irreversible and ironbound. Time is the substance I am made of. Time is a river that carries me away, but I am the river; it is a tiger that mangles me, but I am the tiger; it is a fire that consumes me, but I am the fire. The world, alas, is real; I, alas, am Borges.

NOTE TO THE PROLOGUE

All expositions of Buddhism mention the *Milinda Pañha*, an apologetic work from the second century, which relates a discussion between the King of the Bactrians, Menander, and the monk Nagasena. The latter reasons that as the King's chariot is not the wheels, nor the body, nor the axis, nor the pole, nor the yoke, neither is man matter, form, impressions, ideas, instincts, or consciousness. He is not the combination of those parts nor does he exist apart from them. After a controversy that lasts for many days, Menander (Milinda) is converted to the faith of the Buddha.

The *Milinda Pañha* has been translated into English by Rhys Davids (Oxford, 1890–1894).

Freund, es ist auch genug. Im Fall du mehr willst lesen,
So geh und werde selbst die Schrift und selbst das Wesen.

Angelus Silesius: *Cherubinischer Wandersmann* (1675), VI, 263.

Epilogue

As I corrected the proofs of this volume, I discovered two tendencies in these miscellaneous essays.

The first tendency is to evaluate religious or philosophical ideas on the basis of their aesthetic worth and even for what is singular and marvelous about them. Perhaps this is an indication of a basic skepticism. The other tendency is to presuppose (and to verify) that the number of fables or metaphors of which men's imagination is capable is limited, but that these few inventions can be all things for all men, like the Apostle.

I should also like to take this opportunity to correct an error. In one essay I attributed to Bacon the thought that God composed two books: the world and the Sacred Scripture. Bacon was only repeating a scholastic commonplace; in St. Bonaventure's *Breviloquium*— a thirteenth-century work—we read: *creatura mundi est quasi quidam liber in quo legitur Trinitas*. See Etiènne Gilson: *La philosophie au moyen âge*, pages 442, 464.

J. L. B.

Buenos Aires, June 25, 1952

INDEX

Abasement of the Northmores, The: 11
Abel: relation of, to Jesus, 91
Abélard, Pierre: 157
Abercrombie, Lascelles: 67, 73
Abrabanel, Judah: 180
Achilles: and symbolism, 36; race of, 109–110; on geometry, 113; mentioned, 106, 159
Adam: nature of, 8, 22–23, 24, 91, 92
Addison, Joseph: 47
Adone: 140, 154
Adrogué: 177
Advancement of Learning: 119
Adversus mathematicos: 185
Aeneid: Roman destiny in, 11; realism in, 43, 52; mentioned, 159, 163, 169
Aeschylus: and Greek drama, 167–168
Aesthetes: philosophy of, 59–60, 79
Agamemnon: 67
Agrippa, Marcus: on proof, 111–112
Ahasuerus: 88
Alain de Lille (Alanus de Insulis): 7
Albertelli: on God-sphere relation, 6, 7
Alfarabi: 76
al-Ghazali, Muhammad (Algazel): 95, 118
Al Kitab: 118
All Aboard for Ararat: 23
allegorism: refutation of, 49, 154–155; vindication of, 50, 51, 155; and novel, 157
Almagest: 93
Alonso, A.: 29
Alp Arslan (Sultan): 75
Amat, Torres: 126
America: literature of, 47, 48; people of, 61, 130
Analysis of Mind, The: 25
Anatomy of the World: 8
Anaxagoras: 178
Anselm: 86, 156
Anthologie raisonnée de la littérature chinoise: 106
Apologie de la Religion Chrétienne: Brunschvieg and Tourneur editions of, 9, 94–95

Appearance and Reality: 112, 186
Appolonius of Rhodes: 66
archetype: nature of, xi, 59, 110–111; plan of, 17; as a book, 66–67; and painting, 95
Argentina: language of, 26–30 *passim*; literature of, 64; history in, 131–132; Indians of, 132
Argentine: individualism of, 33, 34, 35; and Spain, 34; on universe, 34, 166; on ethics and philosophy, 166; mentioned, 161
Aristotle: relation of, to Adam, 8; on movement, 106, 110; on archetype, 110; on divinity, 112; followers of, 123, 156; on Greek drama, 168; mentioned, 7, 84
Arms and the Man: 165
Arnobius: 95
Arnold, Matthew: 124
art: and music, 5, 66–67; revelation of, 15–17; reality of, 52, 114; and conscience, 60
Artagnan, Charles de Baatz d': 31
Arthur, King: 159
Artigas, José Gervasio: 28
Ascasubi, Hilario: style of, 29, 64, 143
Asclepius: 7
Asoka, King: 151
astronomy. SEE Copernicus, Ptolemy
Atalanta: 124
Attar: pantheism of, 69
author: copying of, 13; and precursors, 57, 108; opinion on, 59; aims of, 60; 60; and contemporaries, 61; and characters, 44, 53, 88, 164–165. SEE ALSO literature
Autobiography: 125
Avicenna: belief of, 76; mentioned, 118
Azcárate, Patricio de: 110
Azorín: 44

Bacon, Francis: on books of God, 119, 189; mentioned, 8, 13, 87 n.
Ballad of Reading Gaol, The: 80
Balzac, Honoré de: effect of, 31

Banda Oriental: 142, 144
Barbarossa: 159
Barbusse, Henri: 67
Barlaam and Josaphat: 151
Barlaams Saga: 151
Baronio, Cardinal César: 151
Batz, Philipp: 92
Baudelaire, Charles: 68, 83, 140
Beatrice: symbolism of, 49, 99, 100, 155; meeting of, with Dante, 97–98, 100
Becher, Johannes: 13
Beckford, William: life of, 138; Hell of, 139, 140
Beckh, Hermann: 153
Bede, the Venerable: 15, 16, 158
Bellay, Joachim du: 41
Belloc, Hilaire: 88, 138
Benda, Julien: 50
Beowulf: 162
Bergson, Henri Louis: 20, 114, 171
Berkeley, George: idealism of, 173–174, 175, 181–182, 183, 184; God of, 182; mentioned, 124, 171
Bestiary: 161
Betrachtung: 108
Bhagavad-Gita: 69
Biathanatos: suicide in, 89–92
Bible, the: and science, 23–24; aesthetics vs. theology in, 59; suicide in, 90–91; oral-written relation in, 117; interpretation of, 119–120, 128
Bibliographical Institute of Brussels: 103–104
Bibliothèque Orientale: 140
Biography of the Infinite: 109
Bion of Borysthenes: 37
Blake, William: 83, 124
Blanqui, Louis Auguste: 23
Bloy, Léon: and Kafka, 108; on universal history, 120; on symbolism, 125–127, 128; on self-knowledge, 162; mentioned, 80
Bluntschli, Johann Kaspar: 165
Boccaccio, Giovanni: 157
Boethius, Anicius: 156, 185
Bolívar, Simón: biography of, 138
book: burning of, 3–5; as sacred, 5, 46; characteristics of, 118, 163, 164. SEE ALSO Bible; literature; Sacred Scripture, the
Book of Rites: 4
Book of the Splendor: 44
Boswell, James: 81, 144
Bradley, Francis H.: on infinite regres-

sion, 112–113; on time, 186; mentioned, 20, 123, 156, 181
"Brahma": 69
Brethren of Purity: 76, 118
Breton Cycle: 160
Bridge Builders, The: 34
Bridges, Robert: 122, 123
Britons: battles of, 159; mentioned, 161
Brooklyn Eagle: 71
Brooks, Van Wyck: 65
Brown, John: 68
Browne, Sir Thomas: as conceived in sin, 22; on divinity, 94, 119–120
Browning, Robert: 84, 107, 108
Bruno, Giordano: xi, 8, 93
Brut: 158–161 *passim*
Buddha: teachings of, 148 n., 152, 187; effect of reality on, 149, 152; canonization of, 151
Buddhacarita: 151
Buenos Aires, Argentina: language in, 29; Hitlerites in, 134; and Gaucho, 144
Bunyan, John: 85, 144
Burton, Sir Richard Francis: 145
Buscón: style in, 39, 142
Buti, Francesco da: 98
Butler, Samuel: 165
Byron, George Gordon: 68, 112

Cabrera, Luis Gerónimo de: 161
Caedmon: revelation of verses of, 15–16
Caesar, Julius: on memory of mankind, 116; mentioned, 66, 165
Calderón de la Barca, Pedro: 76, 77
Calogero: 6
Calypso: 67
Cambridge History of English Literature: 138
Camöens, Luiz de: 66
Campanella, Tommaso: 8
Cansinos-Assens, Rafael: 13, 24
Cantor, Georg: 114
Capelle, Wilhelm: 110
"Carcassonne": 108
Carceri d'invenzione: 140
Carlyle, Thomas: and author-character relation, 44; on universal history, 46, 120; on fascism, 132; on biography, 137, 138; idealism of, 180; mentioned, 13, 76
Carr, Sir Robert: 89
Carriego, Evaristo: 31–32

Góngora, Luis de: symbolism of, 37; on dream-theatre relation, 47; on plot-story relation, 66
Good Samaritan, the: 38
Gosse, Sir Edmund: on Adam, 24; on Whitman, 67; mentioned, 23
Gosse, Philip Henry: 22–25 passim
government: relation of, to religion, 38
Gracián, Baltasar: 66, 164
Grahame, Cunningham: 145
Grammar (Royal Spanish Academy: 102
Gregory the Great: 146
Griechische Denker: 116
Grimm's Fairy Tales: 84
Groussac, Paul: on Rosas, 28; on Cervantes, 44; on Americans, 61
Guerra, Aureliano Fernández: 37, 38
Guide to Socialism: 178
Guide to the New World: A Handbook of Constructive World Revolution: 129–130
Güiraldes, Ricardo: 143
Gutiérrez, Eduardo: 48, 64, 143

Hakonarson, Hakon: 151
Hamilton, Count Anthony: 140
Hamlet, Prince: 90, 93, 168
Hamlet: infinite regression in, 45; plot-character relation in, 53; mentioned, xii
Hannibal: 3
Han Yu: 106
Hardy (Indologist): 150–151
"Harlot's House, The": 80
Harris, Frank: 86, 165
Hashishin, sect of: 75
Hassan ben Sabbah: 75
Hawthorne, Nathaniel: relation of, to Salem, 48; relatives of, 48, 49; effect of ancestors on, 48, 49; and dreams, 48, 62–63; effect of Puritanism on, 48, 51, 59; seclusion of, 49; physical characteristics of, 49; imagination of, 51, 61, 64; reasoning of, 51; relation of novels of, to stories of, 53, 61; relation of, to Melville and Kafka, 56; influence of Christianity on, 58; opinion of, on writers, 59; on theology vs. aesthetics, 59–60; and contemporaries, 61; and reality of self, 63; biographies of, 63, 65; marriage of, 64; death of, 64–65; mentioned, xi
—, writings of: allegorism in, 49, 50; morality in, 51, 60; fantasy in, 51–52;

subjection in, 51–52; terrorism in, 51–52; pantheism in, 52; art vs. reality in, 52; plot-character relation in, 52–53, 61; destruction of past in, 57–58; number of, 63
Hazlitt, William: 74, 148
Heaven: delights of, 16; nature of, 95
Hector Servadac: 87
Hegel, Georg: 33, 71, 88, 181
Heidegger, Martin: 166
Heimskringla: the heroic in, 168–169
Hejira, the: 75
Helen of Troy: 52
Hell: nature of, 95, 97, 99, 135, 139, 140
Henderson, P. A. Wright: 101
Henley (translator): 140
Henry I (England): 71
Henry James: 79
Heraclitus of Ephesus: on universe, 25, 32, 164, 177; pantheism of, 69; as Aristotelian, 123, 156
Herbart, Johann Friedrich: 19
Hercules: 90, 136
Heriman (chronicler): 156
Hermes Trismegistus: 94
Hermetica: 7
Hernández, José: 28, 29, 64, 143
Heterodox Spaniards: 91
Hexameron: 90
Hindus: historical sense of, 18
Histoire Générale des Voyages: 142
Histoires desobligeantes: 108
Historia de la eternidad: 172
Historia ecclesiastica gentis Anglorum: 15
Historia Regum Britanniae: 159
history: abolition of, 3; sense of, 18; and music, 67; viewpoints of, 131–132; as a dream, 148; nature of, 167; mentioned, xiii
—, universal: definition of, 6, 9; repetition in, 23; as a play, 47–48; and soul, 58; and God, 77–78, 92; as a sacred book, 46, 120; existence of, 185. SEE ALSO universe, history of
"History": 58
Hitler, Adolf: precursors of, 132; supporters of, 134, 135; future of, 135–136; mentioned, 129, 130
Hoare, Sir Samuel: 129
Hobbes, Thomas: 114
Hoffman, Ernst Theodor Amadeus: 61
Hogben, Lancelot: 101
Hokusai: 31

Homer: symbolism of, 36, 67; suicide of, 90; mentioned, 147
Horace: 71
Hottentot dialect: 132
House of the Seven Gables, The: 60
Housman, Alfred Edward: 169
How I Found the Superman: 84
Huang Ti: 4
Huckleberry Finn: 142, 144, 175
Hudson, William Henry: on Gaucho, 142–143; and metaphysics, 144; and Banda Oriental, 144
Huellas del Islam: 95
Hugo, Victor: realism of, 64; on Shakespeare, 148; mentioned, 50, 61, 95, 168, 169
Hume, David: on universe, 104; as Aristotelian, 123, 156; idealism of, 174, 175, 176, 181, 183; mentioned, 124, 171, 184
humor: nature of, 165
Huxley, Aldous Leonard: 19, 171
Huysmans, Joris Karl: 140
"Hymn to God, my God, in my sickness": 22 n.
Hypotyposes: 112

Iamblichus: 119
Ibsen, Henrik: 84
Icelanders: 170
idealism: doctrine of, 58, 173–174, 175; age of, 180, 181; reality in, 184
Iliad: 43, 52, 159
"Illo Virgilium me tempore": 159
immortality: search for, 4; of poet, 71–72; reason for, 180
Imola, Benvenuto da: 98
Indian Philosophy: 186
individual, the: and State, 35, 124; and specie, 121, 122, 157
infinite, the: nature of, 95, 109. SEE ALSO eternity
"Inscripción en cualquier sepulcro": 172
Invisible Man, The: 87
Irving, Washington: 48
Isaiah: and foreseeing of future, 11
Island of Dr. Moreau, The: 87, 88
Israelites: 11, 15

James, Henry: sadness of, 11; on past, 12; realism of, 43; on *The Scarlet Letter*, 61; as biographer, 63, 65; mentioned, 118

James, William: on infinite regression, 114; as Aristotelian, 123, 156
Jaspers, Karl: 166
Jerusalén libertada: 154
Jesus of Nazareth (Christ): life of, 15; and Adam, 22–23; symbolism of, 38, 98; and Samson, 90; precursors of, 91; and suicide, 92; on writing, 117; canon of, 134
Jews: on Bible, 119, 128; and anti-Semitism, 130; language of, 146–147, 177; mentioned, 26
Job: 91
Johnson, Lionel: 80
Johnson, Samuel: on writer-contemporaries relation, 61; mentioned, 59, 81, 164
Jonson, Ben: 13, 147
Joyce, James: and unity of word, 12; on characteristics of Eve, 22; on circumvention of time, 67; style of, 74; mentioned, 42, 118
Judah: 92
Jung, Carl: on dream-literature relation, 48, 64; archetype of, 67
Juvenal: 41

Kafka, Franz: principal theme of, 34; symbolism of, 37; compared to Hawthorne, 56–57; on entrance into glory, 84–85; precursors of, 106–108; nightmares of, 109
Kant, Immanuel: x, 114, 123, 156
Kapilavastu: 151
Keats, John: on "Kubla Khan," 15; on poets, 121; on individual-specie relation, 121–122; and nightingale, 124; mentioned, 61
Kepler, Johann: 93
Ker (Germanist): 162
Kierkegaard, Soren Aaby: 107
Kim: 34, 141
Kingsley, Charles: 24
Kipling, Rudyard: principal theme of, 34; compared to Wilde, 79; and English Empire, 83; and Kim, 141–142
"Knightes Tale, The": 157
Knox, John: 132
Koeppen (Indologist): 151, 153
Koran: traditions of, 75; nature of, 118
Krebs, Nicholas de: 109
Kubla Khan: palace of, 14; poem about, 14–17; dream of, 16–17
Kuhn, Dr. Franz: 103

11 n., 114; on reading, 131; on fascism,
132; on rationalism, 133
Ruth the Moabite: 121

Sacred Scripture, the: nature of, 118,
120, 125. SEE ALSO Bible, the; book
St. Albin: 158
St. Ambrose: 90, 118
St. Augustine: on Creation, 24; on Abel-
Christ-Seth relation, 91; on Samson,
91; on silent reading, 117–118; men-
tioned, 158, 178
St. Bonaventure: 189
St. Dominic: 98
St. Francis: 98
St. Jerome: 98
St. Josaphat: 151
St. Paul: 91, 125, 126, 127
Saintsbury, George E. B.: on Beckford,
138, 139, 140; mentioned, 80
St. Thomas Aquinas: 95, 112
Salas, Don José González de: 40
Sale, George: 118
Salillas, Rafael: 27
"Salut au Monde!": 72
Samson: and suicide, 90–91
Samson Agonistes: 91
"Sanhedrin": 178
San Martín, José Francisco de: 134
Saranoff, Sergius: 165
Sartor Resartus: xii, 44
Sassanidae: 66
Satyricon: 141, 142
Saxo Grammaticus: 170
Saxons: battles of, 159, 168–169; myth-
ology and poetry of, 159–160
Scaliger, Joseph J.: 13
Scarlet Letter, The: 53, 59, 60–61
Scheherazade, Queen: 45
Schleyer, Johann Martin: 102
Schopenhauer, Arthur: on self-knowl-
edge, 18–19; on time, 20 n. 2, 185, 186;
on life-dream relation, 21, 148; on life,
57; on theatre-history relation, 58; on
suicide, 90, 92; on universe, 114, 174;
on individual-specie relation, 122; on
theology, 147; on idealism, 174, 175,
181, 182; mentioned, 154, 165
Schwob, Marcel: 79
science: and religion, 23–25 passim; and
language, 39
Scylla: 67
Second Childhood, A: 82
Segismundo: 168

Segundo Sombra: 141
self: refutation of, xiv; knowledge of,
18–19, 32, 162. SEE ALSO soul
Seneca, Lucius: 13, 38, 41, 90
sensation: perception of, 19, 173, 181
Sense of the Past, The: 11–12
"Sentirse en muerte": 172, 178
Sepher Yetzirah: 119
Seth: 91
Seven Pillars of Wisdom: 170
Sexcenta monodisticha sapientum: 171
Sextus Empiricus: 185
Shakespeare, William: effect of, 31; real-
ism of, 43, 45; and Marlowe, 57; char-
acteristic of, 74; magnification of, 147;
relation of, to other men, 148, 178;
mentioned, 21, 36, 42, 50, 76, 124, 165,
177
Shankara: 147
Shaw, George Bernard: on Hell, 135;
self-evaluation of, 165; characters of,
165, 166; basic subjects of, 166; on
plurality in life, 178; mentioned, xiv,
87, 116
Shelley, Percy Bysshe: xi, 10
Shih Huang Ti, Emperor: and Great
Wall of China, 3–5; and destruction of
past, 3–5
Siddhartha: 150–153 passim
Sigurdarson, King Harald: 168–169
Silesius, Angelus: xv, 12 n. 2, 188
Simurg, the: 69, 77
sin: effect of, 8, 139; conception in, 22;
as universal, 34; and heart, 58; exist-
ence of, 135
Sinbad the Sailor: 142
Siris: 182
Sirmond: 95
Smith, Kemp: 171
Society of Jesus, the: 17
Soergel, Albert: 165
Soledades: 66
Solomon: 7
Sombra, Don Segundo: 34, 157
Some Problems of Philosophy: 114
"Song of Myself": 68–70
Sophocles: 36
soul: transmigration of, 17, 37–38, 66, 76,
77; as knowable, 18–19; and theatre,
47; dream of, 47; and universal his-
tory, 58. SEE ALSO self
Soul of Man under Socialism, The: 80
South, Robert: 8
space: wall in, 4; as absolute, 8; dimen-

Tuñón, Enrique González: 26
Tusculanae: 168
Twain, Mark: 131, 142, 144
Twice-Told Tales: 53

Ulysses: 22, 67
Unamuno, Miguel de: 44
universe, the: Ptolemy on, 7; Copernicus on, 8; and Pascal, 8–9; and law of casuality, 23, 112; as eternal, 24–25, 32; order in, 34, 37, 156; outcast of, 56; and atoms, 96, 166; classification of, 104; and God, 104, 147; and philosophies, 114; language of, 119 and n., 125; as cerebral, 174; existence of, 186–187; mentioned, xi. SEE ALSO world
—, history of: knowledge of, 23; as a dream, 58; symbolism in, 125; duration of, 177. SEE ALSO history, universal
Ureña, P. Henríquez: 29
Urizen: 83
Ursprung der griechischen Philosophie: 6
Uspenski, Gleb Ivanovich: 20

Vacarezza (author): 26
Valencia, Gregorio de: 91
Valera, Cipriano de: 126
Valréy, Paul: on history of literature, 10; characteristics of, 73, 74; on Pascal, 93; mentioned, xi, xiv
Valmiki: 45
Van Doren, Mark: 68 n.
"Varia imaginación": 47
Vathek: 68, 137–140 *passim*
Vatican, the: 87
Vedanta: 25, 166
Vereker, Hugh: 79
Verne, Jules: 86–87
Versailles, Treaty of: 134
Victory: 53
Vies chinoises du Bouddha: 152
Vikings: 135
Villamayor, Luis: 27 n.
Virgil: allegorism of, 49, 99; and art-reality relation, 52; and Dante, 97, 98; on founding Rome, 159; mentioned, 76, 155
Visuddhimagga: 186
Vitali (author): 99
Vita nuova: 156
Vitoria, Francisco de: 90
Vives: 13

Volney, Constantin: 71
Voltaire: 81, 88, 139, 140
Vom Nutzen und Nachtheil der Historie: 71

Wace: interpretation of, 158, 160
Wakefield: interpretation of, 53, 54–56
Waley, Arthur David: 111 n.
Watts, George F.: 50
Way of Purity: 186
Weber, Baron Karl von: 163
Weimar, Duke of: 167
Wells, H. G.: on future, 11; on P. H. Gosse, 23; characteristics of writing of, 86–88; on contemporaries, 129–130; and Nazism, 130; on racism, 131
Welt als Wille und Vorstellung: self-knowledge in, 18–19; time in, 20 n. 2, 185, 186; individual-specie relation in, 122; allegorism in, 154; idealism in, 174, 181, 182
West, Rebecca: 79
Western Culture: 135
Whitehead, Alfred North: 17
Whitman, Walt: effect of, 31; and own poetry, 37, 67, 68, 71, 73–74; happiness of, 68, 144; and humanity, 68–69, 69–71; eternalness of, 72; compared to Valéry, 73–74; mentioned, xi, xiv, xv, 13, 83, 135, 169
Widsith: 162
Wieger: 152
Wilde, Oscar: and unity of word, 12; on Japan, 31; symbolism of, 79; syntax of, 79–80; correctness of, 80; and critics and reader, 81; on Wells and Verne, 86; on Siddhartha, 153
Wilhelm Meisters Lehrjahre: 176
Wilkins, John: 101–104 *passim*
William of Occam: 156
William the Bastard: 132
Winternitz, Moriz: 152
Woerterbuch der Philosophie: 101
Wordsworth, William: 41, 51
world: history of, 36; nature of, 58, 114, 115, 130, 182; symbolism of, 128; existence of, 185; mentioned, xii, xiii, xiv. SEE ALSO universe
World and the Individual, The: 45–46, 178
World as Will and Idea, The. SEE *Welt als Wille und Vorstellung*
World of Dreams, The: 15
writing: relation of, to spoken word, 116,

204

117; silent reading of, 117–118 and n.;
credulity of, 131–132
Writings: 89, 154
Wulf, Maurice de: 156

Xenophanes of Colophon: 6, 94 n.

Yacaré: 29
Yama: 149
"Year of Meteors": 68

Yeats, William B.: 42, 67, 74

Zahurdas de Plutón, in fine: 38
Zarathustra: 68, 134, 165
Zeno of Elea: on movement, 106, 109–
110; on world, 114; mentioned, x, 166,
171
Zohar: 44
Zola, Émile: 60